NURO

3 Kids and 1 Alien

A Nuro Story

Yana and Yavo

Nuro: 3 Kids and 1 Alien

ISBN: 978-1-9194108-9-0

First Edition

Contents

1: The Tangle Test

The line for the Clarity Assessment stretched all the way around the Hall of Proper Thinking, which was *exactly* as fun as it sounded.

Nuro stood between two other young Linearians, both standing *perfectly* still, both staring *perfectly* forward, both being *perfectly* boring. He tried to copy them. Staring forward. Standing still.

His foot tapped.

He stopped it.

His fingers drummed against his leg.

He stopped those too.

His eyes wandered to the ceiling, where someone had carved patterns into the stone thousands of years ago. Who had done that? Were they bored too? Did Linearians used to be less... Linearian?

"Next," called the examiner.

The kid in front of Nuro stepped up to the assessment desk. Nuro watched the back of his head, smooth and gray-blue like everyone else's, with a faint glow on his forehead where his thought-patch sat.

The thought-patch was *the thing*. Every Linearian had one: a small, translucent spot where your thoughts became visible. Good thoughts looked like arrows. Clean, straight arrows pointing from A to B to C.

Nuro's thoughts looked like a plate of spaghetti someone had dropped on the floor. ***SPLAT.***

"State your name," the examiner said.

"Krell-7," the kid answered.

"Purpose of assessment?"

"To demonstrate clarity of thought."

"First question: What is the purpose of a door?"

Krell-7's thought-patch glowed. A single arrow appeared, blue and bright: DOOR → ENTRY/EXIT.

"A door allows entry and exit from enclosed spaces," Krell-7 said.

"Correct. Clear. Next question..."

Nuro stopped listening. He already knew how this would go. Krell-7 would answer every question with a single arrow. Maybe two, if he was feeling *wild*. The examiner would nod. Krell-7 would pass. Another successful Linearian, ready to contribute to society in calm, predictable ways.

Nuro's foot was tapping again.

"Next."

Deep breath. Nuro walked to the desk.

The examiner was old. *Really* old. The kind of old where you've seen so many Clarity Assessments that your face has forgotten how to make expressions. She looked at Nuro, then at her tablet, then back at Nuro.

"Ah," she said. "Nuro."

Just "Nuro." No number. His parents had refused to give him one, which was either sweet or weird depending on who you asked.

"You are now eleven years in development," the examiner continued. "This is your fourth assessment attempt."

"Third," Nuro said. "One of those was a practice run."

"There are no practice runs."

"There *should* be."

The examiner's eye twitched. Just slightly. Nuro considered this a victory.

"State the purpose of assessment."

"To demonstrate clarity of thought," Nuro recited. The patch was already warming up. Not a good sign. It was supposed to stay calm until the questions started.

"First question." The examiner leaned forward. "What is the purpose of a chair?"

Okay. Chair. Simple question. Don't mess this up.

CHAIR → SITTING.

That's it. That's all you need. Chair equals sitting. Arrow, done, move on.

But he was already doing ***the thing***.

Chair. Sitting. But wait – people also stand on chairs to reach high things. So chairs are also for *reaching*. Reaching is like climbing. Climbing happens on trees. Trees are made of wood. And chairs are made of wood! So chairs come from trees. Trees grow in forests. Forests are ecosystems. Ecosystems are about *connection*: everything depending on everything else. And speaking of connection, people sit on chairs *together*. Chairs at dinner tables. Families talking. Communities forming. The *purpose* of a chair might actually be *community* –

"Nuro."

He blinked.

The examiner was staring at him. So was everyone else in the hall. The patch on his forehead was doing its full light show: threads of glowing color shooting in *every* direction, looping back, connecting to each other, forming shapes that were *definitely* not arrows.

"The question," the examiner said slowly, "was about chairs."

"Right. Chairs." Nuro tried to grab one of the threads, pull it into a line. "Chairs are for... sitting?"

It came out like a question. The examiner looked at his thought-patch, which was still going nuts, now exploring whether chairs could theoretically be used as very ineffective shields, and if so, what that said about furniture design throughout history.

"**Tangled**," she said. "Again."

She wrote something on her tablet. Probably not "*excellent job, very creative*."

"Next question. What is the function of a –"

"Can I try the chair one again?"

"No."

"What if I –"

"No."

Nuro's shoulders dropped. The rest of the assessment went exactly as badly as you'd expect.

* * *

The Waiting Room for Concerned Parents was gray. Everything was gray. Even the benches were gray, and exactly uncomfortable enough to make you feel like you'd done something wrong.

Nuro sat between his mother and father. Neither of them had said anything yet. His mother's thought-patch showed a single worried line. His father's showed two lines running parallel – the Linearian equivalent of a sigh.

The examiner entered. She was holding her tablet like evidence.

"The results are conclusive," she said. "Nuro's thought patterns remain severely tangled. We've now documented –" she checked the screen, "sixty-three distinct connections from a single question about chairs."

"Sixty-three?" his father repeated.

"Sixty-three." The examiner sat down across from them. "At his age, we expect three. Perhaps four, in cases of mild creativity. Sixty-three is..."

"Unprecedented?" Nuro offered.

"Problematic."

Cool. Great. ***Love*** *that.*

His mother leaned forward. "What does this mean for his placement?"

"It means we need to discuss options." The examiner pulled up something on her tablet. "There is a program. The Straightening Initiative. It's designed for young Linearians whose thoughts have become... disorganized."

Nuro's stomach dropped.

He'd heard about Straightening. Everyone had. It wasn't like therapy or learning new skills. It was something else entirely. They went into your brain and *deleted* the connections. Snipped the threads. Rewired you from the inside out.

Kids came out... *quieter*. They smiled, but not at the same things. They stopped recognizing old friends. One kid in Nuro's sector had come back not remembering he used to love music.

It wasn't help. It was **erasure**.

"What does the program involve?" his father asked.

"Focused exercises. Thought refinement. The *elimination* of unnecessary neural pathways."

Elimination. The word sat in the air like something dead.

"We want to help him," the examiner continued. "Tangled thoughts lead to tangled lives. He'll struggle to find placement. Struggle to contribute. Struggle to –"

"He's right here," Nuro said.

Everyone looked at him.

"I'm sitting right here. You could talk to me instead of about me."

His mother put a hand on his arm. Gentle, but it meant *please stop talking*.

"**Absolutely not**," his mother said. Her thought-patch flared, a sharp spike Nuro had never seen before. "That program is *barbaric*. We're not erasing our son."

The examiner blinked. "It's highly effective –"

"We'll find another way." His mother stood up. "There has to be another way."

His father hesitated, then stood too. "We need time to think. As a family."

* * *

That night, Nuro lay on his bed and stared at his star charts.

Star charts were his current thing. Before that, deep-sea creatures. Before that, ancient architecture.

His room was full of evidence: half-finished models, notebooks with drawings that trailed off mid-page.

His mother called it "enthusiasm." His father called it "phases." The examiner had called it "inability to maintain productive focus."

Nuro called it *the way he thought*. But apparently, he thought ***wrong***.

He turned back to the star charts. Somewhere out there, forty-two light-years away, were planets that weren't Lineara. Planets where maybe, possibly, *different* wasn't a problem to solve.

His finger traced the map until it landed on a small blue dot.

Earth.

He'd read about it. Mostly in old survey reports that nobody else bothered with. Earth was famous on Lineara, or *infamous* rather. It was one of the closest habitable planets to home. Same basic atmosphere. Similar food chemistry: Linearians could use a small food converter to extract the right amounts of fat, protein, and carbohydrates from Earth food and reshape it into something edible. Linearians could actually *survive* there without special equipment.

But they never visited.

Earth was classified as "chaotic but functional", which was Linearian for "*messy and we don't understand it*." Too many species. Too many ecosystems. Plants that grew in *every* direction instead of neat rows. Animals that behaved **unpredictably**. And the dominant species, humans, were somehow even messier. They had art and music and something called "jokes." Apparently jokes involved saying things that weren't true, and then everyone felt *happy* about it.

It sounded completely ridiculous.

His translator implant, standard Linearian tech tucked behind his ear, had picked up enough Earth broadcasts over the years to give him fragments. Strange sounds. Stranger meanings.

It sounded kind of ***amazing***.

Nuro's thought-patch flickered. Earth → distance → could a shuttle get there? → fuel requirements → but what if you found shortcuts? → asteroids have gravitational fields → slingshot maneuvers → theoretically possible → but why would anyone try?

He sat up.

Why would anyone try?

Because maybe, somewhere out there, *tangled* was just... *different*.

* * *

Downstairs, his parents were talking. Nuro wasn't supposed to hear, but Linearian houses weren't built for secrets: straight walls carried sound in straight lines.

"I'm scared for him," his father was saying. "Not the program, I'm not suggesting that. But I don't know how to help him. Sixty-three connections for a question about chairs. How does he function in a world that expects straight lines?"

"He functions *differently*. That's not the same as not functioning."

"But Lineara doesn't have room for *different*. You know that. I want him to be happy. I want him to have a future. And I don't know how to give him that."

Silence.

"He starts everything," his father continued, softer now. "Completes nothing. And I don't know how to prepare him for a world that won't even *try* to understand him. I love him exactly as he is. But I'm terrified that won't be enough to protect him."

Nuro pressed his back against the wall. The glow on his forehead had gone dim.

His father wasn't wrong. That was the worst part. Lineara *didn't* have room for different. The problem wasn't his parents. The problem was this planet.

He looked at his star charts. At the little blue dot.

Maybe he didn't fit here. But what if somewhere out there, *different* wasn't something that needed fixing?

* * *

He didn't *decide* to take the shuttle. Not really.

He just wanted to look at it. The family shuttle was small, old, meant for trips to the supply stations and back. Nothing special.

But it had star charts. And a navigation system. And a full fuel cell because his father was the kind of person who always kept full fuel cells. No tracking beacon, either, too old for that.

Nuro sat in the pilot seat. Just to see how it felt.

He pulled up the navigation screen. Checked the distance. That was all.

He calculated the route to Earth. Not because he was actually going to *go*. He just wanted to know if it was *possible*.

It was. Barely. If he used the asteroid fields for gravitational assists - which normal Linearians would never think of, because normal Linearians didn't think about asteroids and momentum and "what if you fell *around* something instead of toward it?"

But Nuro thought about those things.

He thought about *everything*.

His finger hovered over the launch sequence. His thought-patch was going wild again, fear and excitement and what-ifs spiraling into each other.

His parents loved him. He knew that now, more than ever. They were fighting for him in the only ways Lineara allowed.

But Lineara didn't allow much.

What if there was somewhere that did? Somewhere – someone – who thought lines weren't the only way?

He'd come back. He'd find answers and come back. He just needed to know if *different* could exist somewhere without being a problem to solve.

Nuro pressed the button.

The shuttle hummed.

The roof opened.

And Nuro went ***everywhere***.

2: The Accidental Trip

Space was *very*, *very* big.

Nuro had known this before. He'd studied star charts. Done the math. Understood, intellectually, that the distance between Lineara and Earth was measured in numbers so large they stopped meaning anything.

But knowing and *experiencing* were different things.

The shuttle hummed around him. Stars stretched in every direction. And Nuro was alone in a way he'd never been alone before.

His thought-patch flickered. Scared. Excited. Scared again.

"Okay," he said out loud, just to hear something. "Okay. This is fine. You're fine. You're just... flying through infinite space in a shuttle you technically stole. Borrowed. *Borrowed without asking*. Which is stealing."

Great. Helpful self-talk. Really nailing it.

He pulled up the navigation system. The standard route to Earth glowed on the screen. A long, curving arc. Avoided all obstacles. Followed all regulations. Would take approximately six months.

Six months.

Nuro didn't have six months of food. He hadn't exactly *planned* this.

He'd grabbed emergency rations from the shuttle's storage - enough for maybe a month if he didn't think about taste. The fuel cell was full - his father was the kind of person who always kept full fuel cells, but what good was fuel if you starved before you arrived?

The patch started doing its thing.

Six months → too long → need shorter route → obstacles in the way → asteroids → but asteroids have mass → mass means gravity → gravity can be *used* → what if you didn't go around the asteroids? → what if you went *through* them? → not through-through, that would be bad → but through the field, using their gravity → slingshot effect → faster, not slower → the "obstacles" could be *shortcuts*...

Nuro's fingers moved across the navigation screen before he'd even decided to move them. He wasn't plotting the safe route. He was plotting *his* route. The one that had appeared fully formed while the computer was still calculating.

It looked nothing like the standard path. It zigzagged through asteroid fields. It curved around gas giants. It used gravitational pulls that the computer kept flagging as "inadvisable" and "potentially catastrophic."

But the estimated travel time had dropped from six months to ***three weeks***.

"Huh," Nuro said.

The first asteroid field was ***terrifying***.

Rocks the size of houses tumbled past. Some bigger. Some on fire. The shuttle's warning system screamed at him in three different tones, which Nuro found unhelpful.

But something clicked. He wasn't seeing individual rocks anymore. He was seeing the *pattern*. The flow. The spaces between.

Left. Right. Down. Through the gap that was only a gap for two seconds before it wasn't.

The patch blazed with connections: trajectory, momentum, timing, that rock's spin rate, this rock's shadow meaning another rock behind it –

He shot out the other side.

Silence. Stars. Empty space.

The shuttle was fine. *He* was fine. Somehow.

"That was –" he started, then couldn't find the word. Terrifying? Amazing? *Both?*

He went with: "That was *really* dumb and I should never do it again."

He checked the navigation. The next asteroid field was in four hours.

* * *

By the third asteroid field, he'd stopped being scared.

By the fifth, he was almost ***bored***.

By the seventh, he was doing loops just to see if he could.

He *loved* this. Every obstacle was a puzzle. Every puzzle had patterns. And patterns were what he ***did***.

The standard navigation would have taken him around all of this. Straight lines. Safe distances. No thinking required.

But thinking was the *point*. New problems. New connections. New ways through.

For once, he wasn't the problem. He was the solution.

* * *

The gas giant came up faster than expected.

Nuro had planned to use its gravity – swing around, pick up speed, slingshot toward Earth. Simple physics. He'd calculated it perfectly.

What he hadn't calculated was how ***pretty*** it would be.

The planet filled his entire viewscreen. Swirling colors. Storms the size of Lineara. Bands of orange and red and something that might have been purple, depending on how his translator handled colors.

The glow on his forehead went wild. Storm patterns → wind speed → atmospheric composition → why purple? → light refraction → but also magnetic fields → could the storms be electrical? → that would explain the –

"PROXIMITY WARNING," the shuttle announced.

Nuro snapped back. He'd drifted too close. *Way* too close. The gravity was pulling harder than he'd planned, and he was heading *into* the atmosphere instead of around it.

"*No no no –*"

He grabbed the controls. Pulled up. The shuttle *groaned*.

"Come on, come *on* –"

The planet's edge filled his vision. Beautiful and deadly and absolutely not where he wanted to be.

Full thrust. Everything the shuttle had.

For three very long seconds, nothing happened.

Then the shuttle pulled free. Shot out at an angle he hadn't planned – but still on course.

"Okay," Nuro breathed. "Okay. New rule. Pretty things can kill you. Don't look at pretty things."

He looked at the navigation. Still on track. Three weeks to Earth, if nothing else tried to kill him.

* * *

Earth appeared sooner than expected.

Blue and green and white. Swirling clouds. Patches of brown that might be land, patches of blue that were definitely water.

It looked chaotic. Messy. Completely unorganized.

It looked **amazing**.

His translator implant buzzed behind his ear. Incoming signals: radio waves, broadcast frequencies, something called "internet" that seemed to be everywhere at once. The implant hummed as it began absorbing the data, cross-referencing patterns, decoding meaning from context.

Nuro orbited Earth for almost a full day, letting the implant drink in broadcasts, conversations, music, advertisements, news - anything with language in it. The shuttle's emergency rations tasted like cardboard, but he barely noticed. He was too busy watching the planet spin below him while his implant *learned*.

By the time the implant chimed to signal it was ready, Nuro could speak every language on the planet.

Well. "Speak" was generous. The implant had reverse-decoded the patterns. It knew the words. Whether Nuro could use them correctly was another question entirely.

Nuro's thought-patch lit up with questions. What were those white patches? Why was it spinning? How did anything stay on the surface if it was spinning? Were those *lights* on the dark side? Who lived there? What did they think about? Did their brains go in straight lines or did they –

"ATMOSPHERIC ENTRY IN THIRTY SECONDS," the shuttle announced.

Right. Landing. He should probably focus on landing.

Nuro pulled up the descent protocols. Standard approach: identify landing zone, calculate entry angle, maintain steady trajectory, adjust for atmospheric resistance...

The clouds swirled below him. Such interesting patterns. Each one different. Was that one shaped like a Linearan transport vessel? And that one looked almost like –

"ATMOSPHERIC ENTRY IN TEN SECONDS."

The clouds were really beautiful. He could watch them for hours. Maybe he *was* watching them for –

"ATMOSPHERIC ENTRY NOW."

The shuttle shook. ***Hard.***

Nuro grabbed the controls. Too late. He was coming in too steep. Wrong angle. The shuttle's heat shields were screaming, and so was the proximity alarm, and also possibly Nuro himself.

"*Pull up pull up pull up –*"

He pulled up. Overcorrected. The shuttle spun.

Green below. Blue beside. White everywhere.

A garden. He was heading for a garden. Rows of something growing. A house. A fence. Very specific vegetables.

"*Sorry!*" Nuro yelled at the vegetables. "*SORRY!*"

CRASH.

* * *

Silence.

Then: dirt falling. Metal settling. Something *dripping*.

Nuro opened his eyes. He was sideways. Or the shuttle was sideways. Hard to tell.

Through the cracked viewscreen, he could see plants. Broken plants. *Very, very* broken plants.

"Shuttle," he said. "Status report."

Nothing.

"Shuttle?"

The lights flickered once, then died.

Nuro unstrapped himself. Fell against what used to be the ceiling. Found the emergency hatch. Pushed.

Earth air hit him like a wall. *Warm. Wet.* Full of smells he had no names for.

He crawled out of the shuttle and stood in the wreckage of someone's garden.

Tomatoes. He'd landed on tomatoes. He recognized them from the survey files – a common Earth food crop, red and round and apparently *very* important to humans. One was stuck to his shoe and several more were smeared across the shuttle's side.

His thought-patch did a tired little flicker. Tomatoes → food crop → *cultivated* → someone **grew** these → someone is going to be very upset...

From the house, he heard a door bang open.

"MY TOMATOES!"

Nuro looked at the approaching human. Looked at the destroyed garden. Looked at his broken shuttle that would *definitely* not be taking him anywhere.

His thought-patch flickered one more time: *Maybe I should have planned this* ***better***...

3: The Maple Street Kids

The human running toward him was small. Smaller than Nuro, anyway – though probably a couple years older, maybe thirteen. Brown skin, dark hair pulled back in a ponytail, and an expression that suggested Nuro had done something *very, very* wrong.

"MY TOMATOES!"

She skidded to a stop at the edge of the crater. Her eyes moved from the smashed plants to the shuttle to Nuro to the shuttle again.

"You – that's – those were –" She seemed to be having trouble picking which disaster to address first. "**FIFTY-TWO DAYS!**"

Nuro's translator implant hummed as it worked. *Fifty-two days. A measurement of time. Apparently significant.*

"I'm sorry," he said. "I didn't mean to land on your… tomatoes?"

"Didn't *mean* to?" The girl's voice went up at least three notes. "You crashed a **SPACESHIP** into my **GARDEN**!"

"It's not technically a spaceship. It's more of a shuttle. Short-range transport." Nuro paused. "Although I did take it a very long range. So maybe it is a spaceship now."

This did not seem to help.

"Maya?" A new voice. Nuro turned to see another human approaching, this one moving *much* faster, practically bouncing with each step. Lighter skin, messy brown hair that stuck up in multiple directions, wearing a shirt with some kind of Earth creature on it. "Maya, is that a **SPACESHIP**?"

"It's a shuttle," Maya said through her teeth. "Apparently."

"That's so cool!" The bouncy one – not Maya – was already circling the wreckage. "Is it real? It looks real. Are you an alien? You look like an alien. What's your planet like? Is it far? How fast does this thing go? Can I look inside? What's that glowing thing on your head? Do you eat food? What kind of food? Do you have –"

"Kai." Maya held up a hand. "Stop."

Kai stopped. For about two seconds.

"But it's a ***spaceship***, Maya."

"Shuttle," Nuro corrected automatically.

"It's a shuttle!" Kai repeated, as if this was even better news.

There was a lot happening at once. The garden. The humans. Their different energies. Maya's posture said *angry*, but her eyes kept flickering to the shuttle with something that looked like curiosity...

"Uh, guys?"

A third voice. Nuro turned again. This human was younger than the other two, standing several steps back with his arms crossed. He had the same coloring as Maya – siblings, maybe?

"Guys, there's an alien. In our yard. Standing in our tomatoes."

"We *noticed*, Leo," Maya snapped.

"I'm just saying." Leo hadn't moved any closer. "Shouldn't we, like, call someone? The police? The army? NASA?"

"And tell them what?" Kai asked. "That a shuttle crashed in the garden and the pilot is really sorry about the tomatoes?"

"I am," Nuro added. "Very sorry."

Leo stared at him. "It *talks*."

"Wait." Kai held up both hands. "Hold on. Back up. How are you speaking English?"

Nuro touched a spot behind his ear. "Translator implant. It converts my language into whatever the local dominant species uses."

"That's **AMAZING**." Kai's eyes went wide. "Does it work perfectly? Can it do accents? What happens if you try to say a word that doesn't exist in –"

"Kai." Maya cut him off. "Focus."

"Right. Sorry. It's just really cool."

"*He* talks," Maya corrected Leo. Then she paused. "You are a he, right? Do you have... genders? Where you're from?"

The question had a complicated answer. But his head was still ringing from the crash.

"Yes," he said. "He is fine."

"Cool." Maya nodded once, as if checking something off a mental list. Then her eyes narrowed. "Now. My tomatoes."

The tomatoes, it turned out, had been a project.

Not just any project. A *documented* project, with daily measurements, growth tracking, a spreadsheet (Nuro's translator provided: *organized data storage*), and photographs from every angle.

Fifty-two days of work. Crushed under an alien shuttle in approximately three seconds.

"I was going to enter them in the county fair," Maya said. She was sitting on the back porch now, the three humans lined up while Nuro stood in front of them like he was on trial. "I had a whole system. Soil pH. Water schedules. Sunlight tracking."

"She really did," Kai confirmed. "It was intense. There were graphs."

"There were ***beautiful*** graphs." Maya's voice cracked. "Last year I won second place with my carrots. *Second*. I was going to do **better** this time."

Graphs. He'd done something like that once with star formations. Actually, that had been really interesting – wait, focus.

"I'll... help you grow new ones?" he offered.

"Tomatoes take *months*!" Maya's voice cracked. "The fair is in **three weeks**!"

Nuro didn't have a good answer for that. On Lineara, if you damaged someone's property, there were official forms and restitution schedules. He didn't think Earth had those. And even if it did, he didn't have anything to give.

"Why are you here, anyway?" Leo asked. He still hadn't moved from his spot at the far end of the porch. "Like, why Earth? Why *our* yard?"

"I didn't choose your yard specifically. The landing was..." Nuro searched for the right word. "Uncontrolled."

"You crashed," Leo translated.

"I prefer 'uncontrolled landing.'"

"You crashed."

"...Yes."

Kai leaned forward. "But why Earth? Where did you come from? What's it like there? Are there other aliens? Have you been to other planets? What's –"

"Kai." Maya put a hand on his arm. "Let him answer one thing before you ask twelve more."

Kai sat back. Bounced slightly. Clearly it was taking effort.

Nuro took a breath. Where to start?

"I'm from a planet called Lineara. It's... far. Very far. And it's very different from here." He looked around at the messy garden, the uneven fence, the three humans who were all different sizes and colors and energy levels. "On Lineara, everything is organized. Straight lines. Clear categories. Predictable patterns."

"That sounds *nice*," Maya said.

"That sounds *boring*," Kai said at the same time.

Leo just watched. Still suspicious.

"It's... both," Nuro admitted. "But for me, it was mostly a problem. Because I don't think in straight lines."

He tapped his forehead – the spot where his thought-patch glowed.

Maya's eyes went wide. "What *is* that? It keeps... *swirling*."

"It's a thought-patch. Everyone on Lineara has one. It shows how your mind is processing information." Nuro hesitated. This was the part where people usually looked at him differently. "Mine is... tangled. That's what they call it. Most Linearians think in single threads. A to B to C. Mine goes everywhere at once."

He expected the same reaction he always got. The frown. The concern. The *oh, that must be hard for you* voice.

Instead, Kai shot up from his seat.

"Wait. *Wait wait wait*." He was staring at Nuro's forehead like it was the most incredible thing he'd ever seen. "So that glowy thing – those are your *actual thoughts*? Right now? In real time?"

"Yes?"

"And they look like that? All tangled and connected and going in every direction?"

"Yes. That's the problem."

"That's not a problem!" Kai was practically vibrating. "That's ***AMAZING***!"

Nuro blinked. "It... is?"

"Dude. *DUDE*." Kai turned to Maya. "Maya. He thinks in every direction at once. Like – that's exactly what mine feels like! When I'm trying to focus on homework but then I think about the homework and that makes me think about pencils and pencils are made of wood and wood comes from trees and trees are like the lungs of the planet and then I'm researching deforestation for two hours and I forgot about the homework entirely!"

Maya sighed. "We know, Kai. We've met you."

"But I can't *see* it!" Kai gestured at Nuro's head. "He can see it! It's right there! The tangled thing!"

"The tangled thing is considered a malfunction on my planet," Nuro said carefully. "They wanted to fix it. Straighten it out. That's actually why I left."

Kai's excitement dimmed slightly. "Fix it how?"

Nuro didn't want to explain Straightening. Not in detail. "It's... not a good process. They erase the connections. Rewire how you think. People come out of it different. Quieter. They forget things they used to love."

The porch went silent.

Even Leo looked less suspicious now. More... thoughtful.

"That's ***horrible***," Maya said quietly.

"So you ran away?" Kai asked. "To find somewhere that doesn't want to fix you?"

"To find somewhere that doesn't think I need fixing." Nuro shrugged. "Or at least to find out if somewhere like that exists. Earth was listed in the old records as 'chaotic but functional.' I thought maybe..."

He trailed off. This was the part he hadn't thought through. What was his actual plan? Land on Earth, walk up to random humans, and ask them if tangled brains were acceptable here?

Although... technically, that was exactly what he'd just done.

"Chaotic but functional," Maya repeated. She almost smiled. "That's one way to describe it."

"So what happens now?" Leo asked. He'd finally moved closer – just a few steps, but closer. "You're stuck here, right? Your shuttle's trashed."

Nuro looked back at the wreckage. The shuttle was half-buried in dirt, one side crumpled, smoke still trickling from something internal.

"It's… not going anywhere soon," he admitted.

"Where would you even go?" Kai asked. "If you can't go home because they want to fix you, and your shuttle's broken, and you're on a planet where nobody knows you exist…"

"Kai," Maya said. "Not helping."

"I'm just thinking out loud!"

"You're thinking out loud about how he's stranded and alone and –"

"I'm processing! This is how I process!"

He recognized that. The need to say things out loud to understand them. The way thoughts had to escape or they'd overflow.

"I do that too," he said quietly.

Kai stopped mid-argument. "You do?"

"The out-loud thing. When there's too much happening in here –" he tapped his head, " – it helps to let some of it out. Even if it sounds messy. Even if it doesn't make sense yet."

Kai stared at him. Something shifted in his expression.

"My dad calls it '*scattered*,'" Kai said. "Teachers say I need to '*focus*' and '*stay on topic*.' I don't really do that."

"Neither does mine."

They looked at each other.

"Okay," Maya said, standing up. She had her organizing voice on – Nuro could tell even without knowing her well. "Here's what's going to happen. We're not calling the police or the army or NASA, because that seems like a terrible idea for everyone involved."

"Agreed," Kai said quickly.

"We're not telling Mom, because she'll freak out, and Dad's out of town until next week."

"Also agreed."

"Besides," Kai added, "the neighbors are used to weird stuff in our yard. Remember Dad's solar panel experiment? The one that looked like a satellite dish crossed with a greenhouse?"

"The neighbors stopped asking questions after the giant windmill phase," Leo muttered.

Maya almost smiled. "Exactly. One more weird metal thing in the garden? Nobody will look twice."

"And we're not leaving an alien stranded in our destroyed garden with no plan and no shelter."

She looked at Nuro. Then over the fence into Kai's backyard – Maya's family lived next door to Kai's, their yards sharing a wooden fence. In the far corner of Kai's yard sat a treehouse, half-built and clearly abandoned mid-project. It was hidden from both kitchen windows by a big oak tree.

"Kai, your treehouse. Is it stable?"

Kai brightened. "Mostly? I stopped working on it when I got into robotics. But the floor's solid. *Probably*."

"Good enough." Maya turned back to Nuro. "You can stay there for now. We'll figure out the shuttle later. And –" she glanced at the tomato wreckage, " – you owe me."

Nuro nodded quickly. "I owe you."

"Good." Maya started walking toward the house, then stopped. Turned back. "I'm Maya, by the way. That's Kai. The suspicious one is my brother Leo."

"I'm not *suspicious*," Leo said. "I'm *cautious*. There's a difference."

"Sure there is." Maya almost smiled. "And you are…?"

"Nuro," he said. "Just Nuro."

"Well, *Just Nuro*." Maya's almost-smile became a real one. Small, but real. "Welcome to Maple Street. Try not to crash into anything else."

4: Everything Connects to Everything

The treehouse was... *interesting*.

Half of it was solid. Good boards, proper nails, even a window cut into one wall. The other half was more of a suggestion. Boards stuck out at angles. A ladder leaned against one side, unattached to anything.

Kai had brought up supplies: a sleeping bag, a pillow, some granola bars (which Nuro could run through his food converter – a small device from the shuttle's emergency kit that extracted nutrients from Earth food and reshaped them into something his body could digest), and a baseball cap.

"For your forehead," Kai explained, tugging the brim. "In case you need to go outside. Neighbors might ask questions about the glowy swirly thing."

Nuro put on the cap. It felt strange but not bad. **Hidden.**

"I was really into construction for a while," Kai said, gesturing at the treehouse. He didn't seem embarrassed. Just factual.

Nuro felt his thought-patch flicker, then looked at Kai. "How long is 'a while' on Earth?"

"Like, three months? Then I got into robotics."

"And then?"

Kai shrugged. "Astronomy. But only the black hole stuff. Regular stars are **boring**."

Nuro nodded. He understood this *completely*. On Lineara, this would be called "**scattered focus disorder**." Here, apparently, it was just called "Kai."

"Okay." Maya climbed up the ladder with a notebook. She'd found a clipboard somewhere. It had color-coded tabs. "If we're going to fix your shuttle, we need a plan."

"A plan is good," Nuro agreed. He pointed at her clipboard. "I like your... word-holding rectangle."

Maya stared at him. "My clipboard?"

"Is that the word?" Nuro frowned. "My translator sometimes picks... unusual descriptions."

"***Word-holding rectangle***," Kai repeated, delighted. "I'm calling it that forever now."

"Step one: assess the damage." She wrote it down in neat letters. "Step two: identify the parts we need. Step three: figure out where to get those parts. Step four –"

"Your wheel-circles!" Nuro was already at the window, looking down at a bicycle leaning against a tree. "The rotation principle could –"

"Nuro. Step one."

"But the bicycle! The way the gears transfer energy – if we adapted that mechanism, we could redistribute the thrust vector in a completely different –"

"We're on step one." Maya tapped her clipboard. "The ship. The damage. **Focus**."

Right. Concentrate. He could do this. He'd done it before. ***Probably.***

He looked at the shuttle. It sat in the crater where the tomatoes used to be, looking sad and slightly tilted.

Okay. Damage. What was damaged?

The hull had a dent on the left side. That connected to structural integrity. Structural integrity connected to atmospheric pressure. Pressure connected to the air he was breathing right now. Earth air. Which was different from Lineara air. More... wet? Was that a thing? Humidity. That connected to weather patterns. Weather patterns connected to why Earth had clouds and Lineara didn't. Clouds were made of water. Water was in the garden hose coiled by the fence. Garden hose. Flexible tubing. His shuttle's fuel lines were rigid. What if they were flexible instead? What if –

"Nuro."

He blinked. Everyone was staring at him.

"Did you just stand there for two minutes?" Leo asked.

"No. I was thinking about the damage."

"You were staring at the garden hose."

"It's ***connected***!"

Leo's face said it wasn't connected.

Maya sighed. "Okay. Let's try this differently. Nuro, what specific parts of your ship are broken?"

Nuro tried to remember. The landing had been... fast. Loud. Full of vegetables.

"The navigation console had sparks. That's probably not ideal."

Maya wrote it down. "Navigation console. Good. What else?"

"One of the stabilizers is bent. And the fuel intake might be clogged. With **tomato**."

"**Tomato**," Maya repeated flatly.

"They got ***everywhere***."

"I noticed."

Kai was already climbing down the ladder. "We should look at the actual ship, right? See what we're working with?"

"That's step one," Maya confirmed. "Thank you, Kai."

They climbed down. Leo stayed in the treehouse for a moment, studying the shuttle through the window. He had a small notebook in his back pocket – the kind with graph paper. He'd been sketching the shuttle's shape since yesterday, trying to figure out how it worked. Not the jumping-around way Nuro thought. The other way. Piece by piece.

He followed the others down.

The shuttle was **worse** than Nuro remembered.

Up close, the dent was actually a ***series*** of dents. The navigation console wasn't just sparking – it was dark and slightly **melted**. One of the stabilizers wasn't just bent. It was ***completely missing***.

"Where's the other one?" Maya asked, looking around the garden.

"I think it's in the compost bin," Leo said. "I saw something shiny in there earlier. Curved metal, about this long." He held his hands apart, showing the size.

Kai sprinted toward the compost bin. Leo pulled out his graph-paper notebook and started sketching the damage - the dents, the melted console, the gap where the stabilizer should be.

Nuro tried to concentrate on the damage too. But the garden hose by the fence kept catching his eye. And the bicycle. And the neighbor's solar panels. Solutions kept appearing, connecting, branching -

"Nuro." Maya was watching his forehead. "You're doing the thing again."

He blinked. "What thing?"

"The swirly thing. Where you stop talking but keep thinking."

Kai came back holding a very dirty stabilizer. Leo had filled half a page with careful sketches.

"The hose could fix the fuel lines," Nuro said. "And the bicycle gears could help with thrust conversion. And –"

"One thing at a time," Maya said. "Please."

Leo looked up from his notebook. "That's not focus. That's **random**."

The word hit Nuro in the chest.

Random. Not connected. Not logical. Just noise.

His thought-patch dimmed. He could feel the threads pulling back, shrinking, going quiet.

"It's not –" He stopped. The words wanted to come out all at once. "The bicycle and the hose and the – they're all part of –"

He couldn't find the thread to pull.

"Then explain it," Maya said. "In order. Start to finish."

He tried to find the beginning. But there wasn't one. The bicycle led to the hose led to the solar panels led to the shuttle led back to the bicycle. It was a web, not a line.

"I... ***can't***. Not in order."

Maya's face softened slightly. But she still looked frustrated. "Then how is anyone supposed to **follow** it?"

Nuro didn't have an answer.

Kai was watching him. His face had a look Nuro couldn't read.

"Maybe," Kai said slowly, "we just need to figure out how to **translate**."

"Translate what?" Leo asked.

"Nuro-brain to regular brain." Kai shrugged. "He's seeing stuff we're not. We just need to find a way to ***catch up***."

Maya snorted. "Or he could just explain things properly."

"Maybe **proper** varies from brain to brain."

They all stood there. The shuttle sat broken in the crater. The stabilizer dripped compost onto Kai's shoes. The bicycle gleamed in the afternoon sun.

Nuro's thought-patch flickered weakly. He wanted to explain. Wanted to show them the connections he saw. But every time he tried, the words came out tangled too.

Maybe that was the problem. Maybe it wasn't just his thoughts that were broken. Maybe it was ***all of him***.

5: The Worst Helper

Nuro wanted to be useful. He ***really, really*** did.

The problem was that "useful" kept meaning something different than he expected.

The first few days were rough. But on Day Three, things got **interesting**.

* * *

Day Three: Kitchen Help

Kai's mom was making cookies. She seemed nice. She hadn't actually seen Nuro up close yet – just a wave from across the yard. Kai said she was "busy with work stuff" and "not really paying attention." Still, Nuro kept his baseball cap on, just in case.

"Nuro wants to help," Kai announced. "He's really good at... um... ideas."

Kai's mom smiled. "Sure! You can help measure ingredients. The recipe's right here."

Recipe. Instructions. **A to B to C.**

Nuro could do this.

"Two cups flour." He measured flour. Got most of it in the bowl.

"One cup sugar." He measured sugar. Some spilled, but that was fixable.

"One teaspoon vanilla."

He opened the vanilla. It smelled ***amazing***. Like something warm and secret.

"What else smells like this?" he asked.

"What?"

"The vanilla. What connects to this smell?"

Kai's mom looked uncertain. "I don't... cinnamon, maybe? Some people think they complement each other."

Cinnamon. Nuro had smelled cinnamon somewhere. Kai's sock drawer? No, that was something else. The spice cabinet. He'd seen it earlier.

"Can I add cinnamon?"

"The recipe doesn't call for –"

But he was already reaching for it. Just a little. The flavors *connected*.

"And what about this?" He'd found a jar of something bright red.

"That's paprika. That definitely doesn't go in –"

"But the color! It matches the brown of the cookie dough. **Warm colors.** They're *all* warm colors."

"Nuro, sweetie, color isn't how recipes work."

He added a shake of paprika anyway. And some of the black pepper next to it, because it had an interesting smell. And a squeeze of lemon juice, because citrus brightened everything.

The cookies came out of the oven.

The cinnamon ones were **amazing**. Kai ate three before they cooled.

The paprika-pepper-lemon ones were… ***not***. Kai's mom threw them out while making a face like she'd bitten a battery.

"Some worked!" Nuro said hopefully.

"Some isn't really the goal with recipes," Kai's mom said gently.

* * *

That Night

Nuro was in the treehouse. Alone. The others were inside, eating the non-paprika cookies.

He could hear them through the window. Kai's mom had left. Just the three kids now.

"He means well," Maya was saying.

"I know." That was Leo. "But he's kind of... **useless**? He can't do anything *normally*."

"Leo."

"What? It's true. He puts pepper in cookies. Everything he touches gets **weird**."

Silence.

"He's *nice*," Leo added, like that made it better. "He's just... he doesn't work the way **things work here**."

Nuro pulled back from the window.

His thought-patch had gone dim again. The threads that usually sparked and connected were just sitting there. *Quiet.* **Still.**

He found his idea notebook. One of Kai's old school notebooks, barely used. Nuro had been filling it with sketches, observations, thoughts that might be useful.

He turned to a blank page. Wrote:

Earth brains are straight too.

They match shapes. Follow recipes. Stay on ***step one.***

I don't fit anywhere.

He stared at the words. They looked lonely on the page.

In the distance, the kids laughed about something. The sound drifted up to the treehouse. *Warm and easy and* **together**.

Nuro closed the notebook.

6: Kai's Confession

Nuro couldn't sleep.

The treehouse was quiet. The neighborhood was quiet. Even his mind was quiet, which almost never happened.

He lay on the pile of blankets Kai had brought up and stared through the unfinished part of the ceiling. Stars were visible. Lots of them. Earth's sky was messier than Lineara's - more stars, more colors, more everything.

Somewhere up there, past the mess, was Lineara. Straight lines and single threads and citizens who never folded checklists into birds.

He wondered if his parents had noticed he was gone yet.

Probably. Definitely. They'd noticed, and they were worried, and they were probably talking to the Council right now. "Our son has run away. Please don't Straighten him. We'll find him. We'll fix this."

Fix this. Fix him.

The ladder creaked.

Nuro sat up fast. But it was just Kai, climbing through the gap in the floor. He was wearing pajamas with rockets on them and carrying a flashlight.

"You're awake," Kai said. Not a question.

"Stars."

Kai looked up. "Yeah. Good stars tonight." He sat down next to Nuro, leaving a careful space between them. "You were looking toward Lineara."

Nuro didn't ask how Kai knew which direction that was. He'd probably researched it already. Kai was like that.

"I was thinking about home," Nuro admitted.

"You want to go back?"

The question sat there for a moment. Did he?

"At least there, they expect me to be broken," he said finally. "Here, everyone seems surprised when I mess things up. There, they already know. ***Less disappointment.***"

Kai picked at a splinter in the floorboard. He didn't say anything for a while.

"You're not broken," he said eventually.

"You heard Leo. I can't do anything normally."

"Leo's twelve and thinks he knows everything. I'm thirteen and I *definitely* don't."

"He's not wrong, though." Nuro looked at his hands. "I matched puzzle pieces by '*feeling*.' I put pepper in cookies. I can't stay on step one because steps two through **ninety-seven** keep appearing in my head."

Kai laughed. A short, surprised sound.

"What?"

"Nothing. Just –" He shook his head. "Come with me."

Kai's room was at the back of the house. He led Nuro through a window – easier than the door, apparently – and across to his closet.

"Okay." Kai opened the closet doors. "Look."

Nuro looked.

The closet was full. Not of clothes. Of things. Objects. Projects.

A guitar leaned against one corner. A nice one, with stickers on the body. Next to it was a ukulele. Next to that was a keyboard with dust on the keys.

"What's that?" Nuro pointed at the guitar.

"Guitar."

Nuro's translator hummed, searching. "My implant says... 'stringed noise-box for recreational sound-making.'"

Kai grinned. "That's the most accurate description of a guitar I've ever heard."

"Played guitar for three months," Kai said. "Got pretty good. Then I wanted to learn ukulele. Then piano. Now they all just... sit there."

He pointed to a shelf. Rock collection. Each rock had a tiny label. "Intense for about six weeks. I can still tell you what kind of rock most of them are. Igneous, sedite - sedimentary - whatever. But I haven't touched them in two years."

Half-finished robot kit. "Was going to build it with my dad. Got most of the way through. Then I found coding and wanted to program my own robot instead."

Telescope. "Astronomy phase."

Coding books. "Lasted longer, actually. But I kept jumping between languages. Learned a little Python. Little JavaScript. Little Scratch. Never got good at any of them."

Basketball in the corner. Chess set missing three pawns. Language learning app icons visible on an old tablet – Spanish, Japanese, French, German.

"Four languages?" Nuro asked.

"Started four. Speak zero. Well, I can say 'where is the library' in Japanese. So that's something."

Kai sat down on his bed. The closet stayed open, all its evidence on display.

"Everyone thinks I can't commit to anything." His voice was flat. Not sad exactly. Just *tired*. "My dad says I'm '**scattered**.' My mom says I have '*so many interests*.'"

He made air quotes around the phrase.

"Teachers say I have '**potential**' but don't '*apply myself*.' Which apparently means I'm smart enough but don't care enough."

"But you learned all these things," Nuro said.

"Barely."

"You learned guitar in three months. You know rock types. You built most of a robot."

Kai shrugged. "Yeah, but I didn't finish any of it. Starting things **doesn't count**."

Nuro thought about that. On Lineara, it definitely didn't count. On Lineara, starting things was nothing. Completing things was everything. A straight line had to have an end or it wasn't a line.

But looking at Kai's closet, Nuro saw something different.

He saw someone who had been excited about sounds, so he learned to make them. Someone who had been excited about rocks, so he learned to name them. Someone who jumped from thing to thing because *everything* was **interesting**.

"On Lineara," Nuro said slowly, "this would be evidence of **malfunction**."

Kai's face tightened slightly. "Here too, kind of."

They sat with that. Two malfunctions *together*.

* * *

"I learn stuff fast," Kai said after a while. "That's the thing. When I'm into something, I pick it up quick. My guitar teacher said I had real talent. My coding teacher said I was ahead of the class."

"But?"

"But then I move on. And everyone acts like the fast learning doesn't matter because I didn't stick with it." He picked at the rocket on his pajama pants. "Like learning is *only* valid if you **finish**. If you get a certificate or a trophy or whatever."

Nuro understood this more than he wanted to.

"On Lineara, I was the same," he said. "Star charts for six months. Deep-sea creatures before that. Ancient architecture. Food preservation on long space voyages."

"Food preservation?"

"It's more interesting than it sounds. The vacuum sealing alone –" He stopped himself. "Anyway. My room looks like your closet. Half-finished models. Notebooks with drawings that trail off. A rock collection I was excited about for eleven days."

"Eleven days?" Kai almost smiled. "That's short even for me."

"They were really nice rocks."

Now Kai did smile. Small, but real.

They sat there. The closet full of started things glowed in the moonlight from the window. Guitar. Ukulele. Telescope. Robot parts.

"What if it's ***not*** a malfunction?" he said.

"What do you mean?"

"I don't know exactly." Nuro tried to organize the thought. It was hard. The idea kept branching. "Just – you learned all those things. Fast. And then moved on. What if that's not broken?"

Kai considered this. "Like... **sampling**? At an ice cream shop?"

"Maybe. You've tasted *everything*."

"But I don't have a **full scoop** of anything."

"Neither do I." Nuro looked at the closet again. "Maya does. Leo does. But *we* don't."

Kai was quiet for a moment. Then he laughed – that surprised sound again.

"What?"

"Nothing." He looked at his closet. At the guitar. At the telescope. "I just never... huh."

He didn't finish. But his eyes were bright.

"I do that too," he said quietly.

"Thinks in tastes?"

"Goes **everywhere** at once. Sees how things connect even when they shouldn't. Jumps before it finishes."

"And on Lineara, that's *broken*?"

"On Lineara, that's about to get **Straightened**."

Kai went still. "What does that mean?"

Nuro didn't want to explain. But Kai was here, in the middle of the night, showing him a closet full of proof that Earth brains could be messy too.

"It's a program. They... *fix* you. Make your thoughts go in lines. But you forget things. You come out... **quieter**." He swallowed. "I knew a girl who came back not remembering she used to draw."

Kai didn't say anything for a long moment.

Then: "That's **horrible**."

"I know."

"Like, *actually* horrible. That's not fixing. That's –"

"**Erasing.** I know."

The stars kept shining through the window. Lineara was out there somewhere. The Council. The Straightening program. Everything Nuro had run from.

"You ***can't*** go back," Kai said firmly. "If that's what's there, you can't."

"I can't stay here either. Leo's right. I don't work the way things work here."

"**Screw** how things work here." Kai stood up. He looked almost *angry*. "You made amazing cinnamon cookies. You see stuff **nobody else sees**. You connect things that nobody else connects."

"I also made terrible cookies."

"Some cookies are going to be terrible! That's **fine**! That's how you find the good ones!"

Nuro blinked at him.

Kai seemed to realize he was yelling. He sat back down. Took a breath.

"Look," he said, quieter. "I don't know if your way is better or worse. But it's *a way*. And it's the **same way** I think."

"I've spent my whole life thinking I was broken. And then you show up, and you're the ***same kind of broken*** as me, and..." He trailed off.

Nuro waited.

"I don't know. It just feels *different*. Having someone else."

Nuro's thought-patch glowed a little brighter. He felt it too. Less alone.

"What if we're not in the *right place* yet?" he asked.

Kai shrugged. "Then we **find** it. Or **build** it."

They looked at each other. Two kids with closets full of started things. Two brains that went everywhere at once.

Two malfunctions.

Together.

7: The Maple Street Mystery

A week after Nuro crashed into the tomato garden, the flyers were everywhere.

Telephone poles. Mailboxes. Store windows. Taped to the community board at the entrance to Maple Street.

MISSING: BISCUIT

The photo showed a medium-sized dog with floppy ears and a slightly concerned expression. Like he knew something was about to go wrong.

"**Three days**," Maya said. She was standing in front of a giant map spread across the Pattersons' dining room table. "He's been missing for three days."

The map had colored zones. Red for "searched thoroughly." Yellow for "searched once." Blue for "searched twice." There was a lot of red. A lot of yellow. Even some blue.

No dog.

Mrs. Patterson was sitting in the corner, holding a cup of tea that had gone cold. Her eyes were red. She'd been crying off and on since Nuro had arrived.

"I don't understand," she kept saying. "We looked *everywhere*. We checked every yard. Every alley. The park. The school. The construction site."

"The construction site is still active," Maya noted. "Loud noises. Dogs don't usually go toward loud noises."

"We checked anyway." Mr. Patterson was pacing by the window. "We've checked everywhere twice."

Nuro stood in the doorway, trying to make himself small. This was a human problem. He shouldn't be here. He wasn't useful for *normal* things.

But he had other ideas.

Missing dog → three days → searched everywhere → but no dog found → so maybe not where dog IS → where would dog GO →

He tried to push it down. Focus. This wasn't his business.

→ dogs follow smells → what smells → food? → they'd checked the restaurant dumpsters → fear? → what would scare a dog →

"Nuro?" Kai was watching him. "You okay? Your forehead's doing the swirly thing."

"I'm fine."

He wasn't fine. He ***couldn't stop***.

→ Mrs. Patterson crying → stress → dogs sense stress → would Biscuit come TO stress or run AWAY → probably away → hiding → but hiding WHERE → what changed recently → construction on Oak Street → loud noises → started last week →

"We're organizing another search party," Maya announced. She'd pulled out a fresh map. "Tonight at seven. I've divided the neighborhood into new zones. Smaller sections, more thorough coverage."

Leo was taping new flyers to a stack of poster boards. His graph-paper notebook was open beside him, filled with a hand-drawn map of every location he'd posted flyers. Check marks. X's for stores that said no. Notes in tiny, careful handwriting.

"Twelve more stops," he said. "Every store on Main Street. I'm tracking which ones actually keep the flyers up." He glanced at his notebook. "So far, forty-three percent take them down within two hours."

Kai was bouncing on his heels. "I can do another loop through the park. With treats this time. And a squeaky toy."

Everyone had a job. Everyone was helping.

→ construction noise → fear → hiding → somewhere **QUIET** → opposite of construction → where hasn't been checked → old library? → closed last month → no one goes there now → quiet → *safe* →

"Nuro."

He blinked. Maya was standing in front of him, clipboard in hand.

"You're zoning out again."

"Sorry. I was –"

"I know. It does that." She checked her list. "Can you take Zone 7 tonight? It's the stretch between Cedar and Birch. You'd be looking behind the garages, under porches, anywhere a dog could hide."

Zone 7. Behind garages. Under porches. That made sense. That was logical.

But he was still stuck on the library.

"Has anyone checked the old library?" he asked.

Maya frowned. "The library? It's closed."

"I know. That's why –"

"It's been closed for a month. The doors are locked. How would a dog even get in?"

"Maybe a window? Or a basement entrance? Older buildings sometimes have –"

"Nuro." Maya's voice had that patient-but-annoyed tone he was getting used to. "We're being **systematic**. Zone by zone, grid by grid. The library isn't in the search area because there's no *logical* reason Biscuit would be there."

"But what if –"

"**Trust the process.**" She turned back to her map. "Zone 7. Seven o'clock. Okay?"

Nuro looked at Mrs. Patterson. She was staring out the window now. Still holding her cold tea.

"Okay," he said.

The search party spread out at seven.

Kai went to the park with his squeaky toy. Leo covered Main Street with more flyers. Maya coordinated from the command center (her word) at the Pattersons' house.

Nuro walked Zone 7. He checked behind garages. Looked under porches. Called Biscuit's name into hedges and crawl spaces.

Nothing.

But he kept getting pulled somewhere else.

The old library was six blocks away. Outside the search grid. Nobody had been inside for a month.

Quiet.

He thought about Mrs. Patterson crying. About the construction noise that had started last week. About a dog who was friendly but nervous, Kai had described Biscuit as "jumpy", running from the loud banging sounds, looking for somewhere safe.

Where do you go when everything is **too loud**?

Somewhere *quiet*. Somewhere *empty*. Somewhere **nobody else goes**.

At 8:15, Nuro finished Zone 7. No sign of Biscuit.

He should go back to the Pattersons'. Report in. Get a new assignment.

Instead, he stood at the corner of Cedar and Oak. The old library was visible from here – a brick building with boarded windows and a faded sign.

The connection was right there. Construction → fear → hiding → quiet → library. It made sense. It ***WORKED***. He could see the thread from start to finish.

But Maya had said trust the process. And the process said Zone 7.

He'd done Zone 7.

Nuro looked at the library again. Then at the Pattersons' house in the distance, lights on, people waiting.

The systematic search would continue tomorrow. And the next day. And the next. Grid by grid. Zone by zone.

Or he could follow ***the tangle***.

8: Following the Tangle

The treehouse floor creaked.

Nuro froze mid-climb. Below him, the backyard was dark. Above him, stars. Between, the sound of someone already up there.

"I *knew* it."

Kai's face appeared over the edge. He was grinning.

"You're going to the library."

"How did you –"

"Your forehead was doing that thing all afternoon. And you kept looking north. The library's north." Kai extended a hand, helped Nuro up the last few rungs. "I'm coming with you."

"You don't have to."

"Dude. You're sneaking out at night to follow a **connection nobody else believes**. Of course I'm coming." He grabbed a backpack from the corner. "I brought supplies. Flashlights. Snacks. Dog treats. Squeaky toy."

"Squeaky toy?"

"Biscuit loves squeaky toys. Mrs. Patterson mentioned it like eight times."

Nuro looked at him. Kai was bouncing slightly, the way he always did when he was excited.

"You really think I'm right about the library?"

"I think you **saw something**. And I think ignoring it would be stupid." Kai shrugged. "Besides, what's the worst that happens? We check an empty building and come home."

The worst that could happen was a lot worse than that. Getting caught. Getting in trouble. Proving that Nuro's tangled thinking was just noise after all.

But the thread was still there. Construction → fear → hiding → library. It made sense.

"Let's go," Nuro said.

The streets were quiet.

Most of the neighborhood had given up for the night. Porch lights on, but nobody outside. The search would start again in the morning.

Nuro and Kai walked fast, keeping to the shadows. Not because they were doing anything wrong, exactly. Just because explaining this to an adult seemed complicated.

"So," Kai said, keeping his voice low. "Walk me through it again. The whole chain."

Nuro started explaining, stress, hiding, quiet places, and Kai actually *listened*. Asked questions. Didn't look confused or annoyed. By the time they turned onto Oak Street, Kai was nodding along.

The library was visible now, dark and quiet at the end of the block.

"That's..." Kai shook his head. "That's actually ***really logical***. Like, it sounds random when you first say it, 'crying leads to library', but when you explain the steps, it makes **total sense**."

"On Lineara, they'd call it *noise*," Nuro said. "Too many steps. Too many jumps."

"On Earth, adults might call it the same thing." Kai started walking toward the building. "But it's **not** noise. It's just a ***different path***."

* * *

The front door was locked. The boards on the windows were solid.

But around the back, there was a basement window. Small. Dusty. And cracked open about three inches.

"Big enough for a scared dog," Kai whispered.

They pushed the window wider. It groaned but opened. Nuro went first, dropping down into darkness.

The basement smelled like old books and dust. His eyes adjusted slowly. Shapes emerged: boxes, shelves, a broken desk in the corner.

Kai landed behind him, flashlight already on. "Hello? Biscuit?"

Nothing.

They moved deeper into the basement. Past rows of forgotten donations. Past water-damaged paperbacks and ancient computers nobody had picked up.

"What if I'm *wrong*?" Nuro whispered. The thread that had felt so solid outside was starting to fray. What if this was just another case of him going *everywhere and nowhere*? What if –

"Shh." Kai held up a hand. "Listen."

Nuro listened.

At first, nothing. Just the building settling. Pipes. The faint hum of the street outside.

Then –

A whimper. *Small.* **Scared.**

Coming from behind a row of metal shelving in the far corner.

They moved slowly. Kai handed Nuro the squeaky toy.

"You found him," Kai whispered. "You should be the one."

Nuro crept toward the sound. His thought-patch was glowing so bright it cast **actual shadows** on the wall. He'd never seen it do that before.

Good thing it was dark. From far away, it probably just looked like a headlamp. *Hopefully.*

Behind the shelves, wedged between two boxes of old encyclopedias, was Biscuit.

The dog looked up. His tail wagged once, uncertainly. He was dirty. Tired. But ***okay***.

"Hey," Nuro said softly. He squeezed the toy. It squeaked.

Biscuit's ears perked up. His tail wagged harder.

"It's okay. We found you."

He squeezed the toy again. Biscuit belly-crawled out from behind the boxes, sniffed Nuro's hand, and then –

Licked his face. Over and over. Like Nuro was the **best thing he'd ever seen**.

Kai was laughing. "Oh man. Oh man. You were right. You were actually ***RIGHT***."

Nuro held Biscuit while the dog wiggled and licked and made happy whining sounds.

He had done the thing. The tangled thing. And it had ***worked***.

* * *

They climbed out the way they came in. Biscuit needed help, he was weak from three days without food, but between them, they got him through the window.

The walk back to the Pattersons' felt different. Lighter somehow.

Kai kept looking at Nuro's forehead. "It's still glowing. Your thought-patch."

"I know."

"It looks ***happy***."

Nuro didn't know thought-patches could look happy. But maybe they could. Maybe he was finally doing something right.

The Pattersons' porch light was still on.

"Ready?" Kai asked.

Nuro looked down at Biscuit. The dog looked up at him, tail still wagging.

"Ready."

They walked up to the door. Kai knocked.

Footsteps inside. The door opened.

Mrs. Patterson stared. Her mouth opened. No sound came out.

Then –

"BISCUIT!"

She was crying again. But different this time. Happy crying. She scooped up the dog, hugged him, kissed his dirty fur.

Mr. Patterson appeared behind her. Then Maya and Leo, running from the kitchen.

"Where – how – where was he?" Mr. Patterson asked.

Nuro took a breath.

"The old library. In the basement. He was hiding from the construction noise."

Everyone stared at him. Then at the dog. Then back at him.

"The *library*?" Maya repeated. "But that wasn't even in the **search grid**."

"I know."

She opened her mouth. Closed it.

"But the library's been closed for –" Mr. Patterson started. "How did you even get *in*?"

Nuro and Kai exchanged a look. The basement window. The breaking and entering. The part that probably counted as trespassing.

But Mrs. Patterson just shook her head, tears still streaming. "I don't care. I don't care *how*. You found him."

She was laughing and crying at the same time, Biscuit licking her face.

Kai caught Nuro's eye. Grinned.

Two malfunctions. And they'd **found the dog**.

9: The Wrong Kind of Right

The next morning, Nuro was **famous**.

Well. Famous on Maple Street. Which was probably the *only* street where an alien could be famous without also being kidnapped by scientists.

Mrs. Patterson had called everyone. Mr. Patterson had posted on the neighborhood message board. By 9 AM, there was a small crowd in their front yard. Nuro stood in the middle of it, Kai's baseball cap pulled low over his forehead, trying not to look at his own feet.

"The library!" Mrs. Hendricks from two doors down was saying. "Can you believe it? Three days of searching, and he was in the library the whole time!"

"How did you even think to look there?" asked Mr. Kim from the corner house. "It wasn't on any of the maps."

Everyone looked at Nuro.

He'd never had this many people looking at him at once. On Lineara, attention usually meant **trouble**.

"I just... *connected* some things," he said. "The construction noise. Dogs running from stress. Quiet places nobody checks."

Kai appeared at Nuro's elbow. He had a plate of celebratory pancakes and was working through his third one. "His brain does this thing where it jumps from idea to idea. Sounds random at first, but it *works*."

The adults were nodding slowly. Some of them had that look – the polite but confused look Nuro was getting used to. But they were also *smiling*.

Biscuit trotted over and leaned against Nuro's legs. His tail was wagging. He, at least, didn't care how Nuro thought.

"Hero of Maple Street!" Kai declared, raising his pancake like a toast. "**Nuro the Dog-Finder!**"

A few people laughed. Someone started clapping. More people joined in.

Something warmed up inside him. Not the anxious swirl – something softer. Almost *happy*.

Maybe this was what it felt like when tangled thinking actually **helped**.

Maya was **not** clapping.

She stood at the edge of the crowd, arms crossed, watching. Her face was carefully *blank*. Which, Nuro was learning, usually meant she was feeling a lot of things she wasn't saying.

When the crowd finally broke up – people heading home, congratulating Mrs. Patterson, patting Biscuit – Maya turned and walked toward her house. Didn't say anything. Didn't look back.

Maya's mom had appeared on the porch at some point. Nuro wasn't sure when. She was talking to Mrs. Hendricks now, glancing toward the crater in her garden, then toward Nuro, then back at the crater. Her expression was hard to read.

Later, Kai told him what happened. With that many neighbors talking, the secret hadn't lasted long. Maya's mom had questions. Lots of questions. But she'd also seen Nuro find Biscuit. Seen the whole neighborhood celebrating. Seen her daughter's face when she realized *different* thinking had worked.

"She said she needs time to process," Kai reported. "But she's not calling anyone. And she said you can stay in the treehouse. For now."

For now wasn't forever. But it was enough.

"What's up with her?" Kai asked, following Nuro's gaze.

"I don't know."

But he kind of did know. He'd seen her face when he explained about the library. The flicker of something that wasn't happiness.

Kai offered Nuro the last of his pancakes. Nuro shook his head.

Something inside him dimmed. The warm feeling from the crowd was fading, **dark edges** creeping in.

He'd found the dog. That was good. That was the *goal*.

So why did it feel like he'd also ***broken*** something?

* * *

He found Maya in her room.

She was sitting at her desk, staring at the search maps spread across the surface. Red zones. Yellow zones. Blue zones. All the places Biscuit *hadn't* been.

"Maya?"

She didn't turn around. "Congratulations. You found him."

"Thanks. Are you... okay?"

A long pause. She still didn't turn.

"I'm not upset." Her voice was flat. Careful. "I just need to *think*."

"About what?"

"About how it **worked**."

She didn't say anything else. Didn't explain. The silence stretched.

Nuro waited. But Maya just sat there, staring at her perfect maps.

He left quietly.

He'd been **right**.

But being right had never felt so ***wrong***.

10: The Fight

Maya found him in the treehouse at dusk.

The sun was setting. Orange and pink through the unfinished walls.

He heard footsteps on the ladder. Maya. She climbed up slowly, her face tight. **Hard.**

"We need to talk," she said.

She didn't sit. Just stood there, arms crossed.

"I've been thinking about it all day. Running your chain in my head. Crying → stress → dogs → noise → quiet → library."

She said each word like it *cost* her something.

"And I can't find the **logic**."

"Because each piece connects to –"

"*You* can see the connections. Great." Maya's voice cracked. "But nobody else can follow them. And that means they're **useless**."

"I found Biscuit."

"This time! With *randomness*!" Her eyes were wet. "Do you know how that feels? I spent my whole life doing things *right*. Following steps."

She was shaking now.

"And you show up with your swirly forehead and your jumping thoughts, and suddenly the **messy way** works better?"

"I'm sorry. I just... I think the way I think. I can't make it go in straight lines."

"Have you *tried*?"

The question hung in the air. Like maybe he just wasn't working hard enough.

"Yes," Nuro said quietly. "For *years*. On Lineara. Exercises. Meditation. Focus training. None of it worked."

"Then maybe..." Maya's voice dropped. "Maybe they were right to want to ***fix*** it."

Nuro's thought-patch went dark. Not dimmed. **Dark.**

"What?"

She didn't take it back.

"Maybe tangled thinking **IS** a problem. Maybe it's just..."

She looked at her feet.

"***Broken***."

The word landed. Sat there. Didn't move.

Nuro stood up slowly. He felt completely still inside. **Empty.**

"I found Biscuit," he said. His voice sounded far away. "With my brain. The brain you just called *broken*."

"Nuro –"

"On Lineara, they wanted to **erase** my thoughts. Delete the connections."

He walked toward the ladder.

"I ran away because I thought Earth was *different*. Maybe here, tangled wouldn't mean broken."

He stopped at the edge. Didn't look back.

"I guess I was ***wrong***."

He climbed down. Maya didn't follow.

The yard was dark. Stars overhead.

Nuro walked. Past the shuttle. Past the house. Past the fence. He didn't know where he was going. Didn't care.

For the first time he could remember, he wasn't making connections. Wasn't jumping. Wasn't doing *anything*.

Maybe that was what **fixed** felt like.

Above him, his thought-patch stayed **dark**.

11: Two Truths

Maya was reorganizing her bookshelf.

This was her stress response. Other people bit their nails or paced or cried. Maya *sorted* things. Tonight, the books were going from alphabetical-by-author to organized-by-subject, then sub-organized by publication date.

It was *very* important. It definitely wasn't avoiding thinking about what she'd said to Nuro.

The knock on her door was soft.

"Go away, Leo."

"It's Kai."

She stopped, a biography of Marie Curie in one hand. Kai never knocked. Kai just *appeared* places, already talking about something unrelated.

"Come in."

He opened the door. Stood there. Didn't bounce.

That was weird. Kai **always** bounced.

"Can we talk?" he asked.

"About what?"

He didn't answer. Just walked over and sat on the edge of her bed. Looked at the books. Looked at her.

"That was **harsh**," he said finally.

Maya's stomach tightened. "What was?"

"What you said to Nuro. About his brain being *broken*. About his planet being *right*."

She wanted to defend herself. To explain. To say that she'd been upset, frustrated, that she hadn't meant it the way it came out.

Instead, she just said: "I know."

"He found Biscuit."

"I know."

"And you told him his brain was **broken**."

"I **KNOW**."

The words came out louder than she meant. She put down Marie Curie. Sat on the floor, across from Kai.

"I know what I said. I know it was wrong. I was just..." She trailed off.

"Upset that his way worked?"

"No. Yes. I don't know." She pulled her knees up to her chest. "I was upset that I spent three days doing everything **right** and it didn't matter. He spent three hours thinking *weird thoughts* and saved the day."

"Weird thoughts found the dog."

"I know that too!"

Kai was quiet for a moment. Which was also weird. Kai was *never* quiet.

"Did you know I almost failed fourth grade?" he asked.

Maya looked up. "What? Why?"

"Not because I was dumb. I understood everything." He picked at a loose thread on her blanket. "But I couldn't do things **the way they wanted**. Teachers said I 'didn't follow the prompt.' Parents had meetings. Words like '*potential*' and '**focus issues**.' Like I was *choosing* to do things wrong."

Maya thought about her color-coded notes. Her numbered lists. The way teachers always *praised* her organizational skills.

She'd never been told her brain was **wrong**.

"Nuro thinks like me," Kai continued. "Meeting him was the first time my brain didn't feel like a ***mistake***."

His voice was harder now. Serious.

"And then you told him his planet was **right**."

Maya's eyes stung.

"I wasn't talking about you."

"You were talking about ***both of us***. You just didn't know it."

The room was quiet. Outside, a dog barked. Probably not Biscuit.

"I didn't mean it," Maya said. "What I said. I was upset and I said the worst thing I could think of."

"That's kind of the problem, though." Kai leaned back. "The *worst* thing you could think of was that his brain was **broken**. That's where your mind went when you were angry."

"Because I knew it would hurt him."

"Yeah. It hurt *me* too."

Maya felt something crack in her chest. She'd known Kai for years. He'd always been the bouncy one, the enthusiastic one, the kid who was interested in everything for five minutes. She'd never thought about what that might feel like from *the inside*.

"I'm sorry," she said. And she meant it.

Kai nodded slowly. "I know. But I'm not the one you need to apologize to."

They sat there for a moment. Maya's books stayed half-organized on the floor. For once, she didn't care.

"His way isn't *random*," Kai said. "It just **jumps** instead of walks. Your mind goes A to B to C. His goes A to M to Q. **Different route, same destination.**"

Maya thought about her search grid. Thorough. Complete. *Useless* for a dog hiding somewhere nobody thought to look.

"We should go find him," she said.

Kai raised an eyebrow. "Yeah?"

"Yeah. I need to apologize. And then..." She looked at her half-organized bookshelf. All those carefully categorized books. "And then maybe we should figure out how to use **different tools together**."

Kai grinned. The bounce was back.

"*Now* you're thinking," he said.

* * *

After he left, Maya didn't go back to organizing. She sat on the floor, surrounded by half-sorted books, and thought about what he'd said.

The worst thing you could think of was that his brain was broken.

She'd said it to hurt Nuro. But Kai was right – that was where her mind had gone. Like "broken" was the word waiting in the wings. *Ready*.

What did that say about **her**?

12: The Ship Problem

Ten days on Earth, and Nuro was at his shuttle.

He'd been there all night. And all morning. The sun was high now, burning the back of his neck, but he didn't move.

Parts were scattered **everywhere**. The navigation console, pulled out and disassembled. The fuel intake, disconnected and cleaned of tomato. The bent stabilizer that Leo had retrieved from the compost bin.

Nothing fit back together.

Every time he tried to reconnect something, his mind would *jump* to another piece, another possibility, another what-if. By the time he circled back to the first thing, he'd forgotten what he was doing.

His thought-patch was still dim. Not completely dark like last night, but quiet. *Tired*.

Maybe that was the solution. Just be tired enough that he stopped jumping.

The shuttle stared back at him. Broken. ***Like him.***

"Hey."

Nuro didn't turn around. He recognized Maya's voice.

"I'm busy."

"I can see that." Footsteps on dirt. She was getting closer. "Can I sit?"

He didn't say yes. He didn't say no.

She sat down anyway. Right there on the ground, next to the scattered parts, **not caring about the dirt** on her clothes.

They stayed quiet for a while. Nuro pretended to study the fuel intake. Maya just watched.

"It won't go back together," he said finally. "I've tried eight different ways. Nine if you count the one where I accidentally electrocuted myself."

"Are you okay?"

"My hand is still tingly. But yes."

"That's not what I meant."

Nuro set down the fuel intake. Looked at the shuttle. Looked at his hands.

"Maybe tangled thinking is just... **all directions at once** and *none of them forward*. Maybe I see how things *could* connect, but I can't make them actually connect. Maybe the connections are just in my head."

"Nuro –"

"You were right." The words came out flat. *Empty*. "About my planet."

He stared at the broken shuttle.

"They wanted to straighten my thoughts because straight thoughts **get things done**. Mine just... *go*." He waved his hand vaguely. "And nothing ever gets **finished**."

Maya was quiet for a long moment.

Then: **"I wasn't right."**

Nuro finally looked at her. "What?"

"What I said last night. It was *wrong*. And *cruel*. And I'm **sorry**."

The apology hung in the air. Nuro wasn't sure what to do with it.

"You were frustrated," he said. "I understand. I made your search feel *useless*."

"That's not –" Maya stopped. Started again. "Okay, yes. I was frustrated. I worked *really* hard on that search grid."

She looked at the ground.

"And then your **jumping mind** found what my **walking mind** couldn't. And I felt *pointless*."

"It wasn't pointless. You covered every *normal* place."

"But you found the *abnormal* one."

"By accident."

"By **thinking differently**."

Something flickered inside him. Just a little. A spark of hope, reaching out, then pulling back.

"About the finishing things," he said quietly. "That part *was* true."

"I wasn't right about **any** part." Maya picked up a piece of the shuttle – some kind of connector, Nuro thought. "I was angry and I said things to *hurt* you. That's not the same as being right."

"Look at this." Nuro gestured at the scattered parts. "I've been out here for hours. **Twelve** different ideas."

He dropped his hands.

"And I haven't *finished* any of them. Because every time I start, I jump somewhere else."

Maya turned the connector over in her hands. "Tell me about the ideas."

"What?"

"The twelve ideas. **Tell me about them.**"

"Why?"

"Because I want to *understand*."

Nuro studied her face. She looked serious. Not frustrated-serious or annoyed-serious. Just... *serious*.

"Okay." He pointed to the fuel intake. "Idea one. The fuel lines. On Lineara, they're rigid. Metal tubes."

He pointed to the fence.

"But what if they were *flexible*? Like that garden hose. Then they could route *around* the damaged areas."

Maya nodded. "Okay. And idea two?"

"Idea two was about the navigation console. It's fried. But I noticed Kai has an old GPS unit in his closet, from his hiking phase, I think? The underlying technology is **similar**. If I could adapt the interface –"

"Hold on." Maya pulled out a notebook from her back pocket. Nuro hadn't noticed she'd brought it. "Can you say that again? *Slowly*?"

She was writing. Taking notes. **Asking questions.**

Nobody had ever asked him to go *slower* before. They usually asked him to **stop**.

"The GPS unit," Nuro said carefully. "The coordinate system is similar to Linearan navigation. Different units, but the same *principle*. If I could translate the interface..."

"What would you need to make that work?"

Something sparked inside him again. **Brighter** this time. Ideas starting to reach out.

"I'd need... well, there's the voltage difference. Earth electronics run on different power."

He felt himself light up inside, ideas **connecting**.

"But Kai's robotics phase - he has converters. And the display would need Leo. He's good with small detail work..."

He trailed off. Maya was still writing.

"What are you doing?"

"**Making a list.**" She looked up. "You've got twelve ideas. I'm putting them in order."

Nuro stared at her.

"You'd... *help* me?"

"We'd help **each other**." Maya set down the connector and held up the notebook. Three pages already. His tangles, translated into *steps*.

"Does this look right?"

Nuro read through her notes. Garden hose for fuel lines. GPS adaptation. Voltage converters from Kai's closet. Each idea he'd mentioned, organized into a **sequence**.

"This is everything I said. But it *makes sense* now."

Maya almost smiled. "**That's the point.**"

"I don't understand how you can follow my tangles," he said quietly. "Nobody's ever been able to follow them before."

"I'm not *following* them. I'm **writing them down**." Maya tapped her notebook. "You say the ideas. I catch them before they *disappear*."

Nuro looked at the notebook. At the shuttle. At Maya.

Something loosened in his chest. Not fixed. Not solved. Just... ***less alone***.

"Okay," he said. "Let's try **together**."

Maya smiled, not wide, but *meant*.

"Okay. Tell me about idea three."

13: The Combination

By the time Kai arrived, Maya had filled three pages of notes.

"What's happening?" He stopped at the edge of the crater, looking at the two of them surrounded by shuttle parts. "Did you guys make up?"

"We made up," Maya confirmed.

"That's great!" Kai was already bouncing. "I was worried because –"

"Come look at this."

Kai bounced over, nearly tripping on a piece of hull plating. "Look at what?"

Maya held up the notebook. "Nuro has twelve ideas for fixing the shuttle. I've been **sorting** them."

"Sorting them?"

"Into categories." She flipped to a new page. "Feasible with available materials. Feasible but needs supplies. *Probably* impossible."

She tapped one item at the bottom.

"And one labeled '**Do not attempt without adult supervision.**'"

"Which one's that?" Kai asked.

Nuro winced. "The one involving redirecting the neighbor's electrical grid."

"That one's a *hard* no," Maya agreed. "But look at this list."

She pointed to the first column, item by item.

"Garden hose for fuel lines. Kai's GPS unit. Kai's power converter." She looked up. "These are **real**, **doable** things."

Kai's eyes went wide. He grabbed the notebook, scanned the list.

"Wait. The GPS idea actually makes sense. I remember how that unit works. The coordinate mapping is basically the same as –" He stopped. Looked at Nuro. "You figured that out by looking at my old hiking stuff?"

"I look at a lot of things."

"Yeah, but you actually **SAW** it. The connection." Kai was bouncing again. "I went through a whole hiking phase and never thought about what GPS actually *does* under the hood."

His face fell slightly. "Only problem: my GPS is like three generations old. The connectors are different from anything modern. We might not be able to plug it into anything."

"What about your power converter?" Maya asked.

"That's from the robot kit. Different voltage. And I think I *lost* one of the cables."

They all looked at the list. Half the items had question marks next to them now.

"So we **improvise**," Nuro said. Something sparked in his eyes. "That's what tangled thinking is *for*, right? Finding paths that aren't supposed to exist."

Maya held up her notebook. Pages of organized notes. Nuro's ideas, sorted into categories.

"This is everything he came up with. I just wrote it down **in order**." She pointed at Kai. "And you learn things *fast*. If we need someone to figure out actual wiring –"

"Twenty minutes if it's interesting."

"**Perfect.**"

Someone was following his tangles. *Multiple* someones. And instead of getting lost, they were turning the tangles into something **usable**.

"Okay," Kai said, setting down the notebook. "Where do we start?"

Maya pointed at the fuel lines. "Nuro, explain the garden hose idea again. In detail."

The garden hose idea was *ridiculous*.

It was also, apparently, **brilliant**.

"So the problem," Nuro explained, kneeling by the shuttle's exposed fuel system, "is that the rigid lines cracked on impact. And they can't bend around the damaged section."

"They're metal," Maya noted. "Metal doesn't bend."

"Right. But what if the lines *weren't* metal? What if they were **flexible**? They'd just... go around the damage."

Kai was already examining the garden hose. "This is rubber. It bends fine. But can rubber handle whatever fuel you're using?"

"Linearan fuel is actually *less* corrosive than Earth gasoline. The issue is pressure. The hose would need to hold up under pressure during thrust."

"How much pressure?"

Nuro told him. Kai's eyes did that thing where he was *calculating* something.

"The hose alone won't work. But –" He ran toward the garage. Came back with a handful of metal clamps. "What if we **reinforce** the connections? Like, the hose is the pipe, but we clamp the joints super tight?"

Maya was already sketching in her notebook. "That could work. But we'd need to test the seal before actual flight."

"We can test with water first," Nuro said. "Same principle, lower stakes."

"I'll get the hose." Kai sprinted off again.

Maya watched him go. "He's *really* good at this."

"He learned plumbing basics during his home repair phase."

"Of course he did."

* * *

Leo arrived at lunchtime.

He stood at the edge of the yard, watching them. Nuro was explaining something about the navigation console. Maya was taking notes. Kai was elbow-deep in a box of electronics from his closet.

"What's happening?"

"We're fixing the shuttle," Maya said without looking up. "Nuro has the ideas. I'm organizing them. Kai's handling the technical stuff."

"Is that... actually *working*?"

"So far." She finally looked at her brother. "Want to help?"

Leo hesitated. He'd been the skeptical one since the beginning. The "that's random" voice. The one who said Nuro couldn't do things *normally*.

But the truth was more complicated than that.

"I don't know what I'd do," he admitted. "I can't do the connection thing like Nuro. I don't learn fast like Kai."

He pulled out his graph-paper notebook. The one he'd been carrying since day one. His hands tightened on it.

"I just... *notice* things. Write them down."

It sounded small when he said it out loud. Maya organized. Kai built. Nuro connected. Leo just... *looked*. And drew. And measured. Because that was how his brain worked: details came at him whether he wanted them or not. The crack in the sidewalk. The uneven spacing of fence posts. The exact shade difference between two supposedly identical paint colors.

Most people found it annoying. *Too much detail, Leo. Nobody cares about that, Leo. Why do you always notice the weird stuff?*

So he'd learned to keep quiet. Draw instead of talk. Let the notebook hold what his mouth couldn't say.

Nuro looked up from the navigation console. Something shifted in his expression – *curious*.

"Show me."

Leo's stomach clenched. Showing the notebook meant showing how he *actually* saw things. The level of detail that made people uncomfortable. The measurements nobody asked for. The observations that were "too much."

But Nuro was watching him. Waiting. Not impatient. Just... *interested*.

Leo handed over the notebook.

The pages were filled with careful sketches. The shuttle from different angles. Close-ups of the damaged sections. Measurements. Notes about which parts looked original versus modified.

"You drew all this?" Maya asked, looking over Nuro's shoulder.

"I was trying to figure out how it worked. The *normal* way." Leo shrugged. "Even when I wasn't sure about… all this. Drawing helps me understand things. So I drew."

Nuro flipped through the pages. Then stopped.

"Leo. This drawing of the stabilizer mount."

"What about it?"

"You drew a **crack** here." Nuro pointed. "I didn't see that. The crack is behind the main damage. *Hidden*."

Leo shrugged. "I noticed it when I pulled the stabilizer out of the compost bin. The mounting bracket has stress fractures."

"If we'd reinstalled it without checking…" Kai started.

"It would have **failed** during thrust," Nuro finished. "The whole stabilizer would have *torn off*."

They all looked at Leo.

"That's not 'just noticing things,'" Maya said quietly. "That's catching something that could have ***killed*** you."

Leo's ears went red. He didn't know what to do with that. People didn't usually thank him for noticing things. They told him to *stop* noticing things.

"I just drew what I saw," he said. Because that was true. He couldn't *not* see it. The crack had been right there, and his brain had grabbed onto it and wouldn't let go until he'd documented it.

He flipped to another page in his notebook. The one with the bent stabilizer. He'd measured the angle – *seven degrees* off center. Something about that number kept nagging at him. Seven degrees. Like his old bike's bent training wheel.

The connection sat there, half-formed, itching at the back of his mind. But he didn't say anything. Big-picture connections were Nuro's thing. Leo just noticed the *pieces*. He didn't know how to make them add up to anything.

He closed that page.

Nuro handed back the notebook. "Keep drawing. Keep noticing. We need someone checking the details **we're too distracted to see**."

Something loosened in Leo's chest. Not *despite* how he saw things. *Because* of it.

He sat down. Opened to a fresh page. The seven-degrees thing was still there, in the back of his mind. Maybe it was nothing.

Or maybe it was *something*, and he just hadn't figured out how to say it yet.

Four distinct minds. **Four** ways of working. *One* shuttle.

* * *

By late afternoon, they had a **plan**.

Maya's notebook was almost full. She'd organized Nuro's ideas into a numbered sequence. Each step had a person assigned to it.

Step 1: Fuel System Overhaul - Flexible hose installation (Kai - technical) - Connection reinforcement (Leo - detail work) - Pressure testing (all - outside)

Step 2: Navigation Adaptation - GPS integration (Nuro - concepts / Kai - wiring) - Interface translation (Maya - documentation) - Coordinate calibration (Nuro - Linearan math)

Step 3: Stabilizer Repair - Structural assessment (Leo - inspection / documentation) - Crack repair at mounting bracket (Leo caught this!) - Reinforcement design (Nuro - ideas / Maya - planning) - Physical repair (Kai - execution)

"This is..." Nuro stared at the list. "This is everything I was thinking. But it **makes sense**."

"Ready to start?" Maya capped her pen.

Nuro looked at the list. His ideas. Her organization. Leo's name next to inspection tasks. Kai's next to building.

"I've never had a list that made sense before."

"**This one's yours.**"

His thought-patch glowed. *Brighter* than it had since the fight.

* * *

They started with the fuel lines.

Kai handled the cutting and fitting. His hands moved fast, confident - he'd picked up the technique from a YouTube video he'd watched during breakfast.

Leo tested each connection. Twist, check, twist again. *Meticulous*. Slow. Exactly what the job needed.

Maya kept the schedule. "Fuel lines done by dinner. Navigation tomorrow morning. Stabilizer in the afternoon."

Nuro floated between them. Answering questions. Making suggestions. Seeing new connections.

"Wait," he said suddenly. "The hose isn't quite right. The **diameter** –"

"What about the diameter?"

He felt the connections clicking into place. Garden hose → diameter → water flow rate → fuel flow rate → thrust calculations → original Linearan specs → difference → *adjustment needed* →

"It's too wide. Too much fuel will flood the intake. The engine would *choke*."

Maya wrote it down. "Can we fix it?"

"We need to restrict the flow. Narrow it down at the end. Like a… a…"

"A **nozzle**?" Kai suggested. "Like on a garden hose sprayer?"

"Yes! *Exactly!*"

"I have one in the garage."

"Of course you do."

* * *

By sunset, the fuel system was **done**.

They tested it with water. No leaks. Pressure held. The nozzle solution worked *perfectly*.

"Whoa," Kai said, watching the water flow through. "We actually **did it**."

"Phase one," Maya corrected. "Two more to go."

But she was smiling. They *all* were.

Nuro looked at the three of them. Maya with her notebook. Kai with engine grease on his forehead. Leo sketching the completed fuel system, already documenting what they'd built.

They stood there in the fading light. The shuttle looked less broken now. Still damaged, but not hopeless. **Fixable.**

Like maybe ***they all*** were.

"Same time tomorrow?" Maya asked.

"Same time tomorrow," Nuro agreed.

Kai was already making a list of things to bring from his closet. Leo was mentally preparing for more detail work.

He smiled.

14: Launch

Day two: Navigation.

Kai had the GPS unit apart on the treehouse floor. Wires *everywhere*. A soldering iron borrowed from his dad's garage. Three YouTube tutorial tabs open on his phone.

"Okay," he said, squinting at the mess. "Signal processing happens here. Nuro's console needs input here."

He tapped both components.

"We just need to make them *talk* to each other."

"Can they talk to each other?" Leo asked. He was holding a flashlight in one hand, his graph-paper notebook in the other, sketching the wiring layout as Kai worked. "That wire's about three millimeters too long, by the way."

"Different languages. But **same alphabet**, kind of." Kai touched two wires together. A small spark. "Ow. Okay, not those two."

Nuro was sketching in his notebook. "The coordinate systems use different base numbers. Earth GPS is base ten. Linearan navigation is base twelve."

"So we need a **translator**," Maya said. She was cross-referencing Nuro's notes with the GPS manual.

"Exactly. Something that converts –"

"I can write that." Kai looked up from the wires. "The conversion algorithm. I did something similar during my coding phase. It's just math."

"You can *write code*?"

"I can *learn* to write code. Again. Give me an hour."

It took him forty-five minutes.

Day three: Stabilizer.

The bent one from the compost bin was beyond saving. They'd repaired the cracked mounting bracket – Leo's sketches had caught that, but the stabilizer itself was too warped to use.

"We need a replacement part," Maya said. "Which we *don't have*."

Leo was flipping through his notebook. All those careful drawings of the shuttle. The bent stabilizer. The angle of the damage.

"What if we **don't** replace it?"

Everyone looked at him.

"I've been looking at these sketches." He held up a page showing the shuttle's profile. "The bend isn't random. It's *consistent*. **Seven degrees** off center."

He stopped. *Seven degrees.* That was what had been nagging at him since yesterday.

He flipped to another page – a drawing of a bicycle with one bent training wheel. The connection clicked.

"When I learned to ride, one training wheel was bent. *Seven degrees*, actually. But I could still ride if I leaned left."

He pointed at the shuttle.

"What if the shuttle just... *leans*? **On purpose?**"

Something clicked inside him. Bent stabilizer → imbalanced thrust → compensating lean → adjusted flight pattern → *actually more maneuverable* →

"That could **work**. If we recalibrate the thrust distribution, the ship would fly lopsided *on purpose*. Like a feature, not a bug."

"Can you do that?"

"I can figure out the math. Maya, can you help me organize the calculations?"

"Already getting my notebook."

* * *

Day four: Integration.

Everything was connected. Fuel lines (rubber and clamped). Navigation (GPS-translated). Stabilizers (one real, one compensated for).

The shuttle looked... *weird*.

It had started as sleek Linearan design. Silver and smooth. Now it had garden hose tubing visible on one side. A GPS unit duct-taped near the cockpit. Scorch marks from Kai's soldering experiments. A slightly crooked silhouette from the stabilizer adjustment.

"It looks like a science fair project that got attacked by a garage sale," Leo observed.

Nuro ran his hand along the hull. Garden hose and duct tape and Linearan metal.

"It looks like ***us***," he said quietly.

Nobody asked what he meant. They all knew.

"Ready to test it?" Maya asked.

* * *

The test happened at dusk.

They'd picked the time carefully. Late enough that most neighbors were inside. Early enough that they could still see.

The shuttle sat in the crater where the tomatoes used to be. Maya's mom had said she'd replant next spring. She'd also said Nuro could take off from the yard anytime he wanted. Finding Biscuit had earned him **permanent vegetable-crushing privileges**.

"Okay." Nuro sat in the cockpit. The controls felt different now – Earth tech mixed with Linearan. Familiar and strange at the same time. "Running system check."

"Fuel pressure?" Maya called from outside. She had a checklist. *Of course* she had a checklist.

"Stable. Slightly lower than original design, but within parameters."

"Navigation?"

Nuro tapped the GPS screen. Earth coordinates converted to Linearan on the fly. "Working. I can see the star charts again."

"Stabilizers?"

He toggled the thrust controls. The ship wobbled slightly, then corrected. "Compensating as designed."

"Then I think we're **ready**." Maya looked at Kai and Leo. "Clear the area."

They backed up to the fence. Far enough to be safe. Close enough to watch.

Nuro took a breath.

He'd crashed this ship by letting his attention wander. By following cloud patterns instead of focusing on landing.

But maybe that wasn't the whole story.

Maybe the crash had led him somewhere he ***needed*** to be.

"Initiating launch sequence."

The shuttle hummed. Different than before: the Earth modifications gave it a slightly rougher sound. Like a cat purring with a cold.

"Three. Two. One."

He pressed the thrust control.

The shuttle **lifted**. Wobbled. Leaned left – the stabilizer compensation kicking in. Then *straightened*.

And **rose**.

Ten feet. Twenty. Fifty.

Nuro circled the backyard once. The controls responded smoothly. The navigation tracked perfectly. The fuel flowed without leaking.

It worked.

He brought the shuttle back down. Landed gently in the crater. Only crushed one remaining tomato stake.

The hatch opened. Kai was already running toward him.

"IT WORKED! It actually worked! You **flew**! We fixed it and you *FLEW*!"

Maya was smiling. *Actually* smiling, not just the polite version. "All systems nominal?"

"All systems nominal," Nuro confirmed.

Leo hung back, but he was grinning too.

They stood there, looking at the hybrid shuttle. Alien metal and Earth improvisation, somehow working together. Ideas that started as *tangles*, written down in **lists**. Some parts built fast, others checked twice.

"I couldn't have done this alone," Nuro said.

"Neither could any of us," Kai said.

Nuro turned to Leo. "You caught the crack that would have **killed** me. And the lean idea made the whole thing *fly*."

Leo ducked his head, but he was smiling. "I guess *slow and careful* has its uses."

They laughed. It felt good. Easy.

The shuttle sat in the crater, ready to fly. Ready to take Nuro *home*.

Home.

The word landed *differently* now.

* * *

Later, in the treehouse, they watched the stars come out.

"So," Kai said eventually. "You can leave *whenever* you want."

"Yes."

"Are you **going to**?"

Nuro looked up at the sky. Somewhere out there, past the mess of Earth's atmosphere, was Lineara. *Straight lines* and *single thoughts* and the Straightening Program waiting for him.

"I don't know yet."

Maya nodded. "That's fair. It's a big decision."

"On Lineara, I'd be going back to... well, you know. The Council. The *assessments*."

He stared at the stars.

"Everything that made me feel ***broken***."

"But your parents are there," Leo said quietly.

Nuro's thought-patch flickered. He'd been trying not to think about *that*.

"They are. And they're probably worried."

He pulled his knees up.

"They **love** me, even if they don't *understand* me. It's complicated."

"Family usually is," Maya agreed.

They sat in silence for a while. The stars kept appearing, one by one.

"Whatever you decide," Kai said finally, "we'll still be **here**. This summer. Next summer. *Whenever*."

"The treehouse isn't going anywhere," Leo added. "I mean, it *might* fall down eventually. The main support beam's got about a fifteen-degree lean. But the yard isn't going anywhere."

Nuro smiled. "Thanks."

"Thank us by making a decision eventually. The suspense is *killing* me."

"*Kai*."

"What? It **is**!"

They laughed again. The shuttle gleamed in the moonlight below.

Tomorrow, Nuro would decide.

Tonight, he just wanted to sit here. With his friends. Under the stars.

Different minds. Different tools. ***Same team.***

15: The Choice

Two weeks after crashing into the tomato garden, the goodbye sleepover was Kai's idea.

"If you're leaving tomorrow, we should do something. Mark the occasion. Send-off. *Whatever*."

So here they were: four kids in a half-finished treehouse, surrounded by sleeping bags and snacks and the faint glow from Nuro's forehead.

"This is a lot of food," Nuro observed. The pile included chips, cookies, three kinds of candy, and something called "pizza rolls" that Kai insisted were essential.

"Sleepovers require snacks. It's the **law**."

"Earth has *strange* laws."

"You have **no idea**."

Maya had brought her notebook. Not to organize anything – just to have it. Leo had brought his graph-paper notebook and a flashlight. Kai had brought his phone, three chargers, and a portable speaker playing music so quietly it was basically just background static.

"So," Maya said eventually. "You decided?"

Nuro looked at his hands. "I think so."

"And?"

"I'm **going back**."

The silence was heavy. Kai stopped mid-pizza-roll.

"To Lineara? Where they want to –"

"I know." Nuro's thought-patch dimmed slightly. "I know what's there. The Council. The *assessments*."

He was quiet for a moment.

"The Straightening Program."

"Then why?" Leo asked. Blunt as always.

"Because my parents are there. And they're **scared** for me."

He stopped. Started again.

"I ran because I didn't know what else to do. But running forever isn't a *solution*." He looked at his hands. "That's just **avoiding**."

Maya nodded slowly. "That makes sense."

"Also, I think maybe things could change. On Lineara. Not *quickly*."

Something flickered inside him.

"But if tangled thinkers keep disappearing, nothing will ever be different. Someone has to stay and be ***different out loud***."

"That sounds hard."

"It will be. But I won't be the same as when I left."

He looked at each of them.

"I know things now. About how **different minds** can work *together*. About how none of us could fix the ship alone."

"You'll tell them that?" Kai asked.

"I'll **try**. They might not listen. But I'll *try*."

They were quiet for a while. The music played. The snacks sat mostly untouched.

Then Kai reached into his backpack.

"I have something for you."

He pulled out a notebook. Not fancy – just a standard spiral-bound, blue cover, already a little bent at the corners.

"It's for your ideas," Kai said. "*All* of them. Even the weird ones."

He grinned.

"**Especially** the weird ones."

Nuro took it carefully. "You're giving me one of your notebooks?"

"I have like thirty. From *various phases*."

Kai shrugged.

"But this one's **new**. You can fill it with whatever your brain does."

"What if my ideas don't go anywhere?"

"Then you'll have a notebook full of ideas that didn't go anywhere. That's still *more* than most people have."

Nuro held the notebook close. Something warm spread through his chest.

"Thank you."

* * *

Maya went next.

She didn't have an object to give. Instead, she pulled out a piece of paper.

"I made you something. It's..." She hesitated. "It's kind of *nerdy*."

The paper was a chart. Rows and columns, carefully drawn with ruler lines. At the top: "TANGLED THINKING TRANSLATION GUIDE."

Down the left side were descriptions of Nuro's thought patterns. "Sudden topic jump." "Connection seems unrelated." "Multiple ideas at once." "Doesn't follow linear sequence."

Down the right side were translations. "Ask: what connected these for you?" "Look for the hidden link." "Pick one to start, save others for later." "The destination might make sense even if the path doesn't."

"It's for whoever you try to explain yourself to," Maya said. "A **dictionary**. Like we talked about."

Nuro read through the chart twice. Then a third time.

"You made this for *me*?"

"I figured... if *I* could learn to follow your tangles, maybe others can too. If they have **instructions**."

"Maya, this is –"

"*Nerdy*. I know. But maybe useful?"

"It's **perfect**."

She smiled, brief, but *genuine*.

* * *

Leo shifted uncomfortably.

"I have something too." He pulled out his graph-paper notebook. The one he'd been carrying since day one. "I wasn't sure if I should give it to you. It's not *new* like Kai's, or **useful** like Maya's."

He opened to the first page. A sketch of the shuttle, crashed in the tomato garden. Then another page – the shuttle from above, with careful measurements. Then the damaged fuel lines. The cracked stabilizer mount. The navigation console with its melted circuits.

"I drew *everything*," Leo said. "The whole time you were here. The shuttle. The repairs. The four of us working."

He flipped to a page near the end.

It showed the shuttle lifting off at dusk. And below it, four small figures watching. One with a swirly forehead.

"I thought you might want to remember what we built. **Together.**"

Nuro took the notebook carefully. Page after page of Leo's observations. All the details Nuro had walked past. All the things a careful, methodical mind noticed that a jumping one missed.

"Leo, this is –"

"It's just drawings."

"It's ***proof***." Something glowed warm inside him. "Proof that different minds working together **actually works**. You documented the whole thing."

He held up the notebook alongside Kai's and Maya's gifts.

"When I show the Council what's possible, I can show them this."

Leo's ears went red. "I just drew what I *saw*."

"**That's the point.**" Núro smiled. "You saw what I *couldn't*."

*   *   *

Nuro looked at the three of them. His first *real* friends. His first **team**.

"On Lineara," he said slowly, "do you know if there are partners? People who think differently working together?"

They shook their heads.

"No. Everyone is supposed to think the *same* way. That's the whole point." He paused. "Straight thoughts, single paths, **no deviation**."

Maya frowned. "So the idea of partnering different thinkers –"

"Doesn't exist. They don't even have *words* for it."

"That sounds..." Maya searched for the word. "**Limited**."

"It *is* limited. And that's what I want to tell them." He held up his gifts: Kai's notebook, Maya's chart, Leo's sketches. "I want to show them what we did."

"Found a dog in a *library*," Kai said. "Fixed a spaceship with a **garden hose**."

"With **four** different minds," Maya added.

Nuro nodded. "*Exactly*."

They sat with that. The music played on. A car drove by somewhere in the distance.

"Same time next summer?" Kai asked.

Nuro's thought-patch glowed **bright**.

Same time next summer.

16: The Return

The flight home felt longer than the flight there.

Nuro used the same route he'd mapped on the way out: asteroid slingshots, gravitational assists, the shortcuts that standard navigation would never approve. But this time was different. He had practice now. He knew which risks were real and which ones just *looked* scary. He wouldn't take useless chances, but he wouldn't ignore good paths just because they weren't *standard* either.

The shuttle hummed through the asteroid fields. His hands moved confidently on the controls. Three weeks to Earth. Three weeks back. The same tangled route that had felt terrifying before now felt like ***his***.

It gave him time to think.

The notebook sat beside him. Kai's gift. Still empty, but full of *potential*. Maya's chart was folded carefully in his pocket. Kai's words echoed in his head.

Different route, same destination.

Lineara grew larger in the viewscreen. Gray and orderly. Grid patterns visible even from space.

Home.

He wasn't sure the word *fit* anymore.

They were waiting for him when he landed.

His parents first – his mother running before the hatch fully opened. She pulled him into a hug. Three heartbeats longer than *regulation* allowed.

"Nuro." Her voice cracked. "We were so worried. The Council said you took a shuttle. They said you might never –"

"I'm okay. I'm back."

His father stood behind her. More reserved, like always. But his hands were shaking.

"You scared us," he said quietly.

"I know. I'm sorry."

His mother pulled back. Looked at him. Looked at the shuttle: the garden hose tubing, the GPS unit, the lopsided profile.

"What happened to your ship?"

"I crashed. And then I *fixed* it." He paused. "With **help**."

Before she could ask more, the Council representatives arrived.

* * *

The Clarity Council chamber was *exactly* as Nuro remembered.

Tall gray walls. Perfect right angles. Seats arranged in **straight** rows. Seven Council members at the front, their thought-patches glowing with single, unwavering lines.

And in the audience: dozens of young Linearians. Brought to watch. To learn. To see what happened to those who *deviated*.

Nuro walked to the center of the chamber. **Alone.**

"Nuro of Sector Twelve," the Head Councilor began. Her name was Vera. Her thought-patch showed one straight arrow, pointing directly at him. "You stole a shuttle. You traveled to an unapproved planet. You have been absent for thirty-one rotations."

"Yes."

"The punishment for shuttle theft is three cycles of restriction. The punishment for unapproved travel is –"

"I know the punishments."

The chamber went quiet. Interrupting the Council was almost unheard of.

Vera's expression didn't change. "Then you also know that your continued... condition... qualifies you for the Straightening Program. Given your flagrant violation of regulations, the Council recommends immediate enrollment."

Nuro felt the old fear rise up. Straightening. Memory erasure. Coming back quieter. Not remembering that you used to love music or connections or wondering what-if.

He took a breath.

"**No.**"

* * *

The silence *stretched*.

"*No*?" Vera repeated.

"I **won't** do the Straightening Program. And I don't think *you* should either."

Murmurs from the audience. Shocked whispers. A few faces showed confusion.

"Then let me show you what I did."

He pulled Maya's chart from his pocket. Unfolded it. Held it up.

"A creature was lost on Earth. The straight-line thinkers searched zone by zone. Three days. Didn't find it."

He pointed to the chart.

"I thought about *crying*. Crying led to stress. Stress led to how frightened creatures behave. Behavior led to **where they hide**. I found it in one hour."

His thought-patch was glowing now.

"That is precisely the *malfunction* –"

"I also crashed my ship." Nuro held up Leo's notebook, open to the sketch of the damaged shuttle. "Because my attention jumped at the wrong moment."

A young Linearan in the back row leaned forward. Their thought-patch was swirling. *Tangled*, like Nuro's.

"But look at this." He turned the pages. Sketch after sketch. The broken fuel lines. The cracked bracket. The garden hose solution. The GPS modification. "A straight-line thinker drew every part. Found a crack I missed. Organized my ideas into **steps**."

He held up Kai's notebook. Empty pages. Full of potential.

"And this – given to me by a tangled thinker. Someone who understood what it's like to be called ***wrong*** your whole life."

He stepped forward.

"The shuttle flew. Look at it. **Garden hose and alien metal.** It shouldn't work."

He let the silence stretch.

"But it *does*."

* * *

Vera stared at him. Her single-arrow thought-patch pulsed once.

"The Council will deliberate."

She stood. The other Council members followed. They filed out through a side door.

The audience sat frozen. Nobody had ever spoken to the Council like that. Nobody had ever refused Straightening *out loud*.

Nuro stood in the center of the chamber, breathing hard.

He'd said it. Everything he'd learned. Everything he believed.

Now he just had to wait.

* * *

The deliberation took two hours.

Nuro sat on a bench outside the chamber. His parents sat with him, his mother holding his hand, his father staring at the wall.

"That was **brave**," his mother said quietly.

"Or *stupid*."

"Sometimes those are the same thing."

His father cleared his throat. "The Council has never changed a Straightening recommendation. Not in forty years."

"I know."

"They may not listen."

"I know that too." Nuro squeezed his mother's hand. "But I had to **try**. And even if they don't listen *today*, maybe someone else will. Later. *Eventually*."

His father was quiet for a long moment. Then he turned to face Nuro directly – something he rarely did.

"The things you said. About different thinking working together. Is that *real*? On Earth?"

"It's real. I **lived** it."

"But how?" His father's voice was tight. Controlled, but barely. "How does it *work*? When your thoughts go everywhere, how does anyone follow? How does anything get **done**?"

Nuro recognized the fear underneath the question. His father wasn't asking about Earth. He was asking about *Nuro*. About years of watching his son struggle. About not knowing how to help.

"I couldn't do it alone," Nuro said carefully. "That's the point. My friend Maya – she thinks in lists. Straight lines. When I had ideas, she wrote them down. Organized them into steps."

"And that... worked?"

"It worked because we were **different**. I saw connections she missed. She caught the steps I skipped over." He pulled out Leo's notebook. "And Leo – he notices details. He found a crack in my shuttle that would have killed me. I'd walked past it a dozen times."

His father stared at the sketches. The careful measurements. The meticulous observations.

"A straight-line thinker," he said slowly. "Catching what a tangled thinker missed."

"And a tangled thinker finding what straight-line thinkers couldn't." Nuro met his father's eyes. "Neither works alone. But **together** –"

"Together you fixed a crashed ship with garden hose." His father's voice was strange. Almost wondering.

"In *days*."

His father's thought-patch, straight and orderly as always, *flickered*. Not just once. Several times. Like something was trying to connect that had never connected before.

"I've spent your whole life trying to figure out how to *help* you," he said quietly. "Maybe I was looking for the wrong kind of help."

"Maybe we both were."

His father nodded slowly. "*Interesting*," he said.

From him, that was almost **enthusiasm**.

* * *

The door opened.

Vera emerged first. Behind her came another Councilor – Thane, Nuro remembered. His thought-patch showed a single rigid line, sharper than the others. He looked *angry*.

"The Council has reached a decision," Vera said. Her face was unreadable.

Nuro stood. His parents flanked him.

"Regarding the shuttle theft: thirty days of community service. Regarding unapproved travel: a formal warning, logged in your permanent record."

Punishment. But manageable. Nuro waited for the rest.

"Regarding the Straightening recommendation..." Vera paused.

"This is a *mistake*," Thane cut in. His voice was sharp. "The recommendation should proceed immediately. One speech does not overturn forty years of –"

"The Council has **voted**, Thane." Vera's tone left no room for argument.

"Four to three is not consensus."

"Four to three is a *majority*." She turned back to Nuro. "The Council has decided to **delay** the program. *Indefinitely*. Pending further observation of the subject's contributions to Linearan society."

Nuro's breath caught. Four to three. Three Councilors had voted to erase his mind *today*.

"Delay? Not *cancel*?"

"The Council is not convinced by a single speech." Her eyes moved to the window, where the patched-together shuttle sat in the landing bay. Garden hose and alien metal. "But the evidence is... *difficult to ignore*. That ship should not fly. And yet it does."

Thane made a sound of disgust. "Rubber tubing and primitive navigation. This proves nothing except desperation."

"It proves *ingenuity*," Vera said quietly. "Which is precisely what the Council has been failing to recognize."

She turned back to Nuro. Her expression hardened.

"You claim tangled thinking can contribute. **Prove it.** You have one year." She folded her hands. "Show us that *different* can be **useful**. Or the recommendation will be reinstated. Councilor Thane will be watching *closely*."

Thane's rigid thought-patch pulsed once. A warning.

It wasn't freedom. It was a trial. A *test*.

But it was also a ***chance***.

"I understand."

"Good." Vera turned to leave. Then stopped. "One more thing. The young one in the back row, with the tangled thoughts."

She glanced toward the chamber door.

"Zix. They have requested to speak with you."

Nuro looked toward the chamber door. A small figure stood there, thought-patch *swirling*.

Zix looked up at Nuro. Eyes wide. *Hopeful*. **Scared.**

Someone like *them*. Standing tall instead of apologizing.

Nuro smiled.

"I'd **like** that."

Summer Continues

Three weeks later, the communicator *crackled* to life.

Nuro had left it behind, a spare communicator from the shuttle's emergency kit. Standard Linearan tech, but he'd rewired it to work with Earth power. One last project before he left.

Kai nearly fell out of the treehouse grabbing for it.

"It's working! Maya! Leo! It's **WORKING**!"

They crowded around the screen. *Static* at first. Then a **familiar face**.

"Hello, *Earth people*."

Nuro was grinning. Behind him, the gray walls of Lineara were visible. But he'd hung something on them, a poster, hand-drawn. It showed four stick figures under a tree. One had a *swirly* forehead.

"YOU'RE **ALIVE**!" Kai shouted.

"I told you I'd be fine."

"You said you'd *TRY* to be fine. That's **different**."

"Fair point. But I'm fine. *Better* than fine, actually."

Maya leaned in. "What happened with the Council?"

"They gave me a year. To prove that tangled thinking can *contribute*." He smiled. "So I started something. A **group**. We call ourselves the ***Tangled Thinkers***."

"A *group*? On **Lineara**?"

"Four members so far. Me, Zix - that's the kid from the chamber - and two others who heard about what I said and *came to find me*."

He shrugged.

"We meet every week. Share ideas. Practice explaining our connections **out loud**."

He looked *happy*. Lighter than they'd ever seen him.

"We ***learn from each other***."

"Is that *allowed*?"

"The Council is 'monitoring' us." Nuro made air quotes. "Which means they don't *like* it, but they can't actually **stop** it because technically we're not breaking any rules."

Leo almost smiled. "*Clever*."

"I learned from the **best**. How are things *there*?"

Kai held up a notebook. It was **full**. Pages covered in sketches, notes, half-formed ideas.

"I'm *actually* writing things down now. Like, **all** of them. Not just the ones I think are good enough."

He flipped through the pages.

"Most of them are *terrible*. But some of them are **okay**."

He grinned.

"And one of them might actually be ***brilliant***? I'm not sure yet."

"That's **perfect**," Nuro said. "That's *exactly* how it works."

Maya's turn. She tilted the camera toward her wall. There was a *new* poster above her desk.

It said: **WHAT IF WE TRIED A DIFFERENT PATH?**

"I made it *myself*," she admitted. "It's not as organized as my usual stuff. But I **like** it."

"It's *beautiful*."

"It's **crooked**."

"It's ***beautifully*** crooked."

She rolled her eyes. But she was *smiling*.

* * *

Leo shuffled into frame last.

"I started a *new* notebook."

He held it up. Graph paper, like always. But the drawings were **different**. Instead of careful observations of *existing* things, there were sketches of things that ***didn't exist yet***.

"I've been *designing* stuff," he said. "Things I want to **build**. I draw them first, figure out how the pieces would fit together."

He flipped to a page showing a complicated structure – part treehouse, part observatory, part something else *entirely*.

"This one's for the backyard. If Kai's parents say yes."

Nuro's thought-patch glowed **brighter**.

"Leo. That's *amazing*."

"It's just drawings. They might not work."

"You're seeing how things could **connect** before you build them. That's not 'just drawings.'" Nuro leaned toward the screen. "That's *planning*. That's your version of what my mind does – except yours actually **makes sense** to other people."

Leo looked at his sketches. Then at Nuro. Then back at the sketches.

"I never thought of it *that* way."

"**Now you will.**"

* * *

The connection was starting to *fade*. Interstellar communication wasn't meant for this distance. But they had a few more seconds.

"Same time next summer?" Kai asked.

Nuro smiled. "**Same time next summer.** I'll tell you how the year goes. You tell me about your notebooks and crooked posters and designs."

"*Deal*."

"**Deal**."

"***Deal***," Leo added quietly.

The screen flickered.

"Goodbye, *Maple Street*."

"Goodbye, **Lineara**."

Static. Then **silence**.

* * *

They sat in the treehouse for a while after. The communicator *quiet*. The summer evening **warm**.

"So," Kai said eventually. "What *now*?"

Maya looked at her crooked poster through the window. Leo flipped through his design notebook. Kai had his notebook open to a **new page**.

"Now," Maya said, "we see what ***different minds*** can do."

* * *

THE END

BOOK 2:

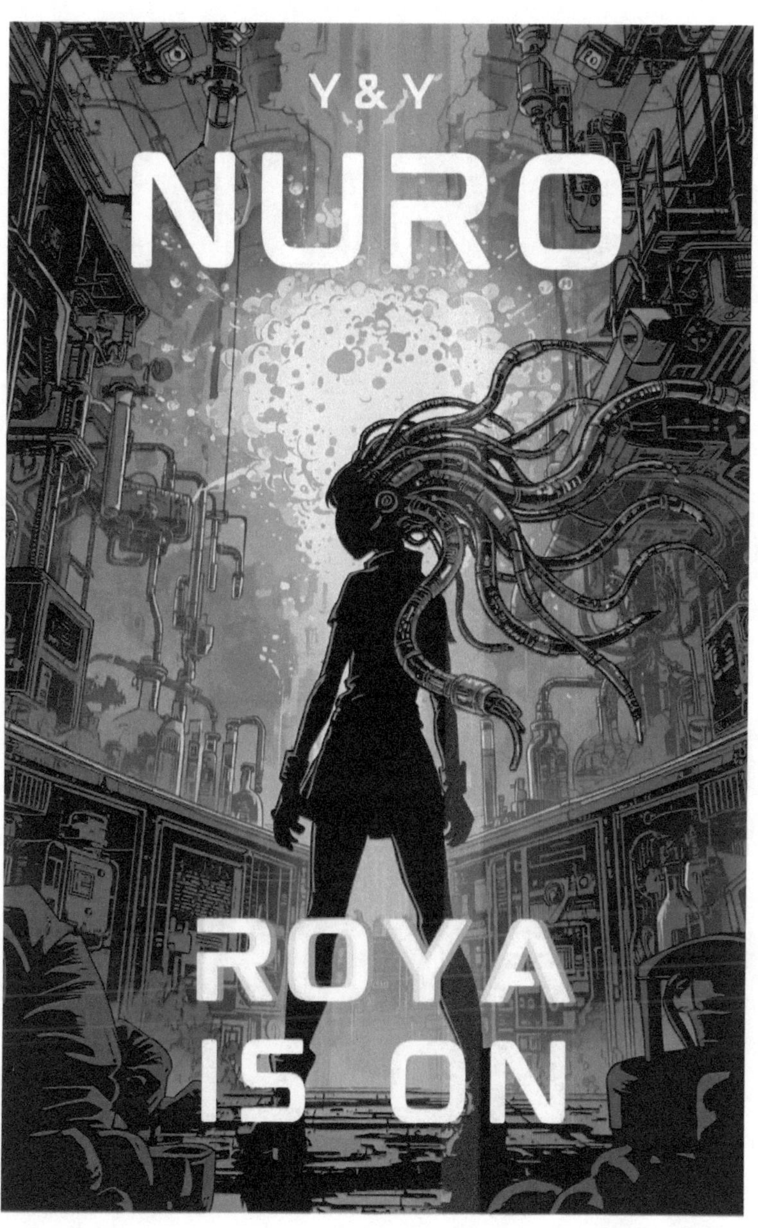

BOOK 3:

www.ingramcontent.com/pod-product-compliance
Lightning Source LLC
LaVergne TN
LVHW091138080826
845145LV00008B/2187